Dorothy Huang's
CHINESE COOKING

Dorothy Huang's
CHINESE COOKING

by Dorothy Huang

edited by Lorry Berce Harju

First edition
1980

PINEWOOD PRESS
Houston, Texas

Pinewood Press
P. O. Box 79104
Houston, Texas 77279

First printing, December, 1980
Second printing, August, 1981
Third printing, December, 1982
Fourth printing, August, 1985
Fifth printing, March, 1990

ISBN 0-9604498-0-9
Library of Congress Catalog Card Number 81-123514

Printed in the United States of America

FOREWORD

Being a long time acquaintance of Dorothy Huang and her lovely family, I was delighted when asked to write this foreword. In the process of formulating my thoughts, a question arose as to what is the uniqueness of Chinese cooking in comparison to American cooking. It is in general agreement among my American and Chinese friends that Chinese cooking emphasizes contrast in color, as well as in texture. Indeed, color (色), aroma (香), and taste (味) constitute the three basic principles of Chinese cooking.

Using these principles Dorothy has taught Chinese cooking for several years in varied settings — from department stores to a university. Her experience in teaching assures the reader who is adventuring into the world of Chinese cuisine that the simplest methods and the best recipes are being offered. Her recipes provide great flexibility. Other features are the accentuation of garnishes and the selection of ingredients which are easily obtained in the United States. With her educational background in nutrition, Dorothy also emphasizes the nutritional aspects in her recipes. For example, overcooking is absolutely to be avoided in order to retain the natural flavor and nutritional value of most foods. The application of cornstarch, wine, and ginger root in cooking meat and seafood assures their tenderness and appetizing aroma. What I find particularly pleasing is that the recipes are almost foolproof; they have been tested over the years both by Dorothy and by her students.

My wife and I have enjoyed Dorothy's cooking on many occasions and I am sure that her recipes will soon become favorites of yours, too.

Beng T. Ho, Ph.D.
Professor
Texas Research Institute of
    Mental Sciences and
    University of Texas
    Health Science Center at Houston

ACKNOWLEDGMENTS

I wish to express my deep gratitude to Lorry Berce Harju for editing the manuscript, to John Semple for providing some of the drawings, and to Beng Ho for writing the foreword. Beng and his wife Daisy also deserve credit for first suggesting that I write this book. Special thanks are due to Linda Posey for offering additional editorial advice; to Ann Criswell, food editor of the Houston Chronicle, for her valuable suggestions; and to my father for the calligraphy on the cover. Also I wish to thank my students in the University of Houston Sundry School for kitchen-testing many of my recipes. Above all, I thank my husband for his constant encouragement and counsel since the book's inception.

CONTENTS

(Cover photograph, **Moo Goo Gai Pan,** *see recipe on page 113.)*

INTRODUCTION

Over the years, many of my students have asked if I had a cookbook that would supplement what they learned from my classes and demonstrations. Finally in 1979, I decided to write a book that would meet the needs of these enthusiastic novices as well as the needs of more experienced cooks. The result is **Dorothy Huang's CHINESE COOKING,** a collection of over 100 of my best Chinese recipes.

Dorothy Huang's CHINESE COOKING includes both dishes used in my classes and additional dishes providing a broader sampling of Chinese foods. Each uses authentic Chinese ingredients, plus fresh meats and vegetables, prepared in a way that maximizes both taste and nutritional values.

I have personally kitchen-tested each recipe numerous times, simplifying the preparation, experimenting with timesaving techniques, and adding interesting variations. In addition, most recipes have been kitchen-tested by my students. Consequently, the instructions are clear and concise, easy enough for the novice yet completely authentic to please the gourmet.

To make cooking easier and faster, most recipes have a prepare-ahead section plus additional tips on storing, freezing, and reheating. Attractive ways to garnish and serve the dish are also mentioned. Other sections of the book give the cook a background in Chinese cooking utensils and methods, special Chinese ingredients, beverages, Chinese menu planning and table settings. These sections will help you add authenticity to your Chinese meals.

I have included popular recipes from different Chinese regions (Canton, Szechwan, Shanghai, etc.) but the book is organized by courses and, in the entrée section, by main ingredients. A detailed index is also included. These features are especially helpful when you have a particular ingredient you wish to use.

The recipes in this book can add taste and nutrition to your diet, variety to your cooking skills, and satisfaction to your time in the kitchen. Whether you are getting your first taste of Chinese cooking or you are already an experienced cook, you are sure to enjoy preparing and eating these delightful dishes.

願君大快朵頤！ (Bon Appétit!)

Houston, Texas   Dorothy Huang
January, 1980

CHINESE UTENSILS

As you begin to explore Chinese cooking, a few Chinese utensils can be very helpful and fun to use. They are available in Chinese specialty stores, gourmet shops, and many department stores.

WOK

"Wok" means cooking vessel in the Cantonese dialect. The wok is a very versatile utensil which can be used for other types of cooking besides Chinese. The traditional conical shape has remained unchanged for centuries; the high sloping sides of the wok make it especially suitable for stir-frying. It can also be used for deep-frying, simmering, and steaming.

Woks come in different sizes; however, the 14-inch diameter wok is ideal for family use. Woks are made of metals such as cast iron, carbon steel, stainless steel, and aluminum. The cast iron and carbon steel varieties are the best since they can retain and distribute high heat evenly; they can also be seasoned or conditioned to improve their performance. Always season a new cast iron or carbon steel wok before its first use.

To Season a New Wok or a Rusted Old One

Wash the wok thoroughly with detergent and hot water; scrub with a scouring pad, if necessary, to remove any factory machine oil or stubborn rust. Rinse and wipe dry. Turn heat to medium, place wok on the range over the metal ring (see next page), and add one teaspoon vegetable oil. Select a stub of unpeeled ginger root that is large enough to hold onto without burning your fingers. Slice the end off the root so that the stub has a fresh surface. Hold ginger root securely and rub oil slowly into the wok. Start in the center and work up the sides of the wok, then back to the center again. When the ginger root turns gray, slice off the gray portion. Keep rubbing occasionally for about ten minutes. Let it cool and wipe with paper towels. Then wash the wok again in hot water with a soft nylon brush or cloth, and dry. Repeat the seasoning process. When a light brown ring forms in the center of the wok, your wok is seasoned.

To Clean and Store the Wok

After you finish using the wok, fill it with hot water for several minutes or just long enough to soften the food particles so they can be removed with a soft brush. (If you let the wok soak for hours or overnight, it will rust very badly.) Rinse and wipe dry with paper towels. Place the wok over low heat for a couple of minutes. Apply a thin coat of vegetable oil to the inside of the wok to prevent rust and keep it seasoned. The wok will eventually blacken with age; this is normal.

Other Types of Woks

Other varieties of woks are available. The **flat-based wok** is like the traditional wok, but has a flat base. It is designed for use on an electric range because it sits right on the heating coils; no wok ring is needed.

Another variation is the **electric wok** with an automatic heat control. The temperature can be set from warm to 425°F. This type of wok is usually lined with a non-stick finish, making it easy to clean and work with. I use it a lot for cooking demonstrations when neither stove nor sink is available.

WOK RING

The wok ring is a recent invention to adapt the wok to an electric range. The wok ring should be sloping, with vents to release heat during cooking. The wok should be set over the larger opening to minimize the distance between the bottom of the wok and the heat source, so you can cook with the maximum amount of heat. The wok can be placed directly on the gas range without the ring.

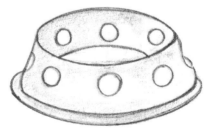

WOK COVER

All woks come with a well-fitted lid, which is primarily used for steaming or braising.

CHINESE SPATULA

The spatula is a partner to the wok. It is flat and wide along the front edge but has a rim on the other three sides. The shape and long handle make it easy to use for stir-frying and scooping up cooked food.

CHINESE LADLE

The ladle looks like a tiny wok with a long handle. You can use any ladle if this tool is unavailable.

CHINESE STRAINER

The strainer is made of brass wire mesh with a long bamboo handle. You may substitute a slotted spoon.

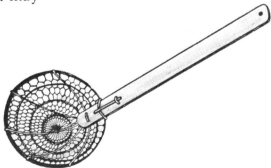

CHOPPING BOARD

The traditional Chinese chopping block is made from the cross-section of a hardwood tree; it is 2 to 6 inches thick and 14 to 16 inches in diameter. You can use a regular wooden chopping board that is large enough to work comfortably.

CLEAVER

The cleaver is a "must" in Chinese cooking. It has a wooden or metal handle, and a broad blade, about 3 by 8 inches, made of tempered carbon steel. It is many tools in one: a knife (for chopping, slicing, shredding, dicing, and mincing); a garlic press; a pulverizer; and a spatula.

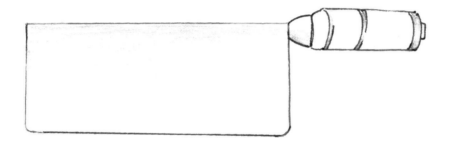

To Use the Cleaver

Hold handle between your palm and the middle, fourth, and fifth fingers, letting your thumb and index finger fall naturally on each side of the blade near the handle.

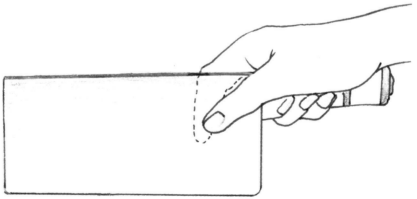

Hold object to be cut with the finger tips of your free hand. Curve the tips of your fingers under so the first knuckles can guide the cleaver blade. To make each cut, lift the cleaver blade barely above the food surface, being careful to keep the blade below the height of your knuckles.

STEAMER

Steamers are cylindrical pots made of aluminum or bamboo.

Aluminum Steamer

For most uses, a 12-inch diameter steamer is ideal. It consists of four parts: the base for holding water; two tiers with holes perforated in the bottom for steam circulation; and a lid to prevent steam from escaping.

Bamboo Steamer

It should be 2 inches smaller in diameter than your wok so the wok can serve as a base for water. The bottoms of the bamboo tiers are woven bamboo lattice, to let steam circulate freely.

Personally, I prefer the aluminum steamer since it does not occupy the wok and is easy to clean. It also lasts longer and comes in handy when you have a big party because the base serves as a large cooking vessel.

Improvised Steamer

Use a wok with lid and a steamer rack or a cake rack. Put the rack in the wok; add water about one inch deep below the rack. When water comes to a brisk boil, place the food in a heat-proof dish on the rack and cover with the wok lid.

CHINESE FIRE POT

The fire pot, a unique cooking vessel, is a covered pot with a chimney rising through the center. The base of the chimney is filled with burning charcoal and chicken broth is poured around the chimney. To cook, dip food in the simmering broth as you would in a fondue pot. You can substitute an electric wok or an electric skillet for the fire pot. See recipe on page 65.

15

CHOPSTICKS

Chopsticks are a versatile tool for the Chinese. They are used not only for eating, but for preparing and cooking foods. They are made of wood, bamboo, plastic, lacquer, bone, ivory, or silver. For preparing and cooking foods, only the bamboo and wooden ones are practical because they are heat resistant.

To Hold Chopsticks

Rest one chopstick between your thumb and index finger about ⅓ of the way down the thick end. Rest the middle of the chopstick on the tip of your fourth finger.

Next, grasp the other chopstick with your middle finger, index finger, and thumb. Keep the tips of the chopsticks even with each other at all times.

Now, widen the space between the tips of the chopsticks about one inch, then close them. Repeat until you can do this easily. If you can achieve a clicking sound, you will be able to pick up food. Remember, dexterity comes with practice.

Chinese Cold Plate

1 Barbecued Pork
2 Abalone
3 Virginia Ham
4 Braised Star Anise Beef
5 Smoked Chicken
6 Braised Star Anise Eggs
7 Sweet and Sour Radishes
8 Cilantro (Garnish)

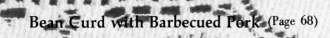

Bean Curd with Barbecued Pork (Page 68)

Stir-Fried Beef with Broccoli (Page 95)

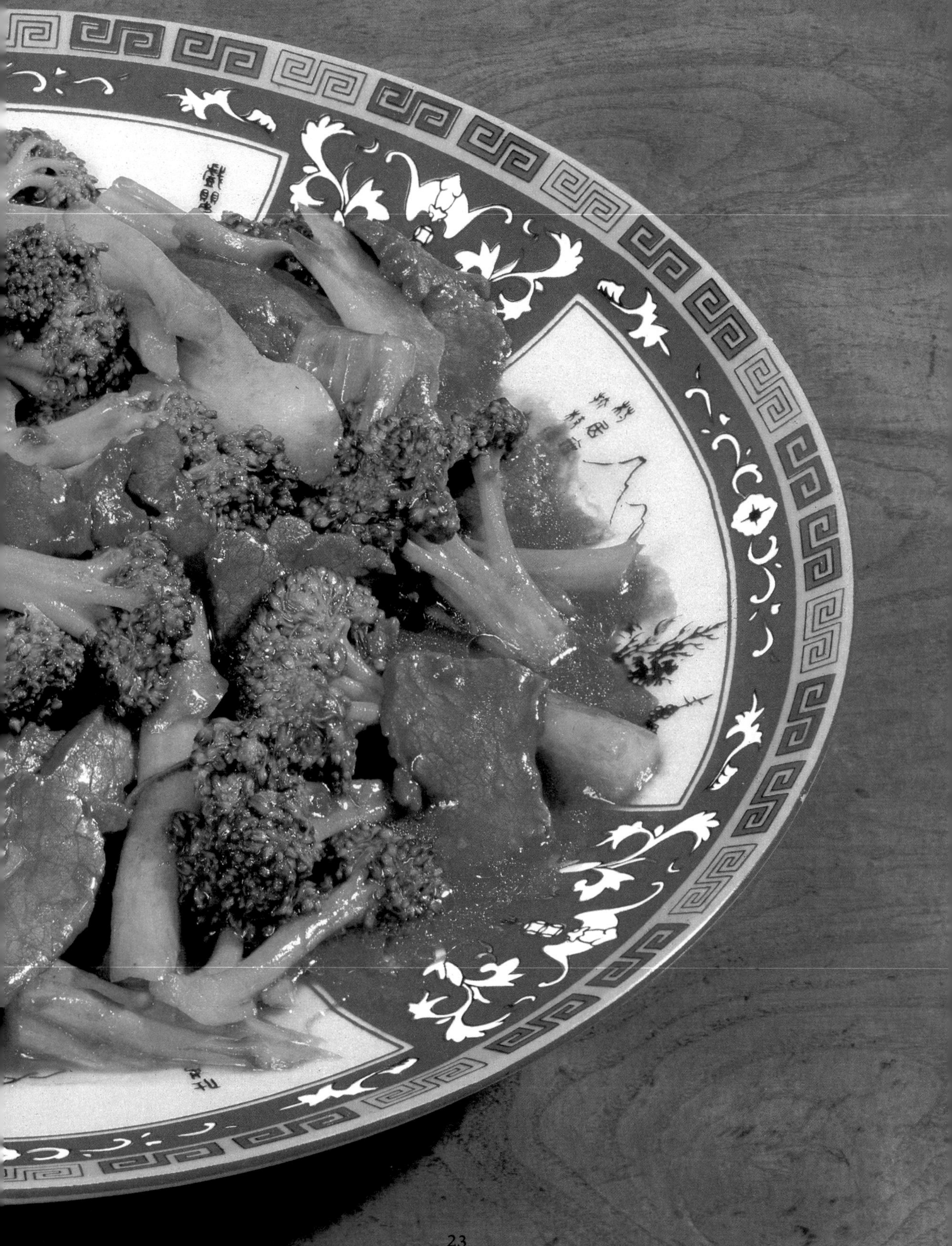

Twice-Cooked Pork (Page 104)

Eight-Treasure Rice Pudding (Page 172)

Chinese Ingredients and Condiments (Pages 33 — 40)

1 Dried shrimp
2 Dried lotus seeds
3 Rock sugar
4 Dried red dates
5 Dried tiger lily buds
6 Black cloud ear
7 Salted or fermented black beans
8 Spiced ginger powder
9 Mustard powder
10 Szechwan peppercorns or Chinese peppercorns
11 Five-spice powder
12 Star anise
13 Preserved black dates
14 Preserved longan pulp

15 Chinese dried mushrooms
16 Bean threads or cellophane
   noodles
17 Hot bean sauce
18 Bean sauce
19 Bamboo shoots
20 Chinese noodles
21 Sweet bean sauce
22 Hot soybean paste
23 Hoisin sauce

24 Plum sauce
25 Gingko nuts or white nuts
26 Water chestnuts
27 Sesame seed paste
28 Barbecue sauce
29 Sweetened red bean paste
30 Abalone
31 Straw mushrooms
32 Birds' nests

33 Oyster sauce
34 Sesame oil
35 Soy sauce
36 Soy sauce
37 Chinese barbecue sauce
38 Sweet or glutinous rice
39 Agar-agar
40 Chinese noodles
41 Purple seaweed or laver

Chinese Ingredients (Pages 33 — 40)

 1 Cilantro or Chinese parsley
 2 Fresh hot pepper
 3 Mung bean sprouts
 4 Wonton wrappers
 5 Ginger root
 6 Dried red chili pepper
 7 Snow peas
 8 Bean curd or Tofu
 9 Egg roll wrappers
10 Winter melon
11 Bok choy
12 Chinese cabbage

CHINESE INGREDIENTS AND CONDIMENTS

Fresh Chinese vegetables are usually available in many big supermarkets, but most of the spices and condiments are found only in Chinese specialty stores.

ABALONE   鮑 魚

Abalone comes precooked in cans. It can be sliced thin and served as a cold plate or stir-fried with vegetables. It just takes seconds to heat; prolonged cooking will toughen it. The canning juice can be used for sauce or diluted as stock.

AGAR-AGAR   洋 菜

Agar-agar is a processed seaweed which comes in dried form. Grayish-white and very light in weight, it is used mainly in cold dishes with shredded vegetables and cooked meat. To prepare agar-agar, soak in tap water, rinse, and squeeze dry. It does not need cooking.

BAMBOO SHOOTS   筍

Sold fresh in China, bamboo shoots are only available in cans locally. After opening, drain the unused portion and cover with tap water. Store in a covered container in the refrigerator, changing the water daily. They will then keep for a week to ten days.

BARBECUE SAUCE   沙 茶 醬

Barbecue sauce made from chili, garlic, soybean oil, fish, dried shrimp, peanut, rice bran, salt, and spice is sold only in Chinese specialty stores. It is available in seven-ounce jars. After opening, cover tightly and refrigerate. It will keep in the refrigerator for months.

BARBECUE SAUCE, CHINESE   燒 烤 醬

Chinese barbecue sauce made from soybeans, flour, sugar, salt, and spices is available in cans or jars. Refrigerate canned sauce in a covered glass jar after opening. It will keep for months if properly stored.

BEAN CURD or TOFU   豆 腐

Bland and fragile, bean curd is made from soybeans. The one that comes in 3-inch squares about 1 inch thick is the firm variety. Refrigerate in a covered container filled with cold tap water, and change the water daily. If freshly made, it will keep for two weeks. Because it is exceptionally high in protein, it is the main ingredient in Chinese vegetarian cooking.

BEAN PASTE, SWEETENED RED　紅豆沙

Sweetened red bean paste is completely different from the bean sauces mentioned later. It is made of puréed cooked red beans and sugar, and is used only in dessert dishes, such as **Eight-Treasure Rice Pudding**. It is sold in nine-ounce or eighteen-ounce cans. After opening, it can be refrigerated in a covered container for two weeks or frozen for months.

BEAN SAUCE or SOYBEAN PASTE　豆瓣醬

Used mainly for seasoning, bean sauce is made from soybeans, flour, salt, sugar, and spices. It is sold in six-ounce cans. After opening, transfer to a covered glass jar. It will keep in the refrigerator for months.

BEAN SAUCE or SOYBEAN PASTE, HOT　辣豆瓣醬

A very important condiment in Szechwan cooking, hot bean sauce contains added chili peppers to give it a hot taste. It is sold in six-ounce cans. After opening, transfer to a covered glass jar. It will keep in the refrigerator for months.

BEAN SAUCE, SWEET　甜麵醬

Used mainly for seasoning, sweet bean sauce is a thick, brownish sauce, made from soybeans, flour, sugar, and spices. It is sold in six-ounce cans. After opening, transfer to a covered glass jar. It will keep in the refrigerator for months.

BEAN SPROUTS, MUNG　綠豆芽

Mung bean sprouts can be refrigerated for two or three days. When ready to use, rinse in a large pot of cold water and drain well.

BEAN THREADS or CELLOPHANE NOODLES　粉絲

Since bean threads are made from mung beans, they are considered a vegetable product rather than a starch. If the recipe calls for deep-fried bean threads, no presoaking is necessary; otherwise soak them in hot water for 10 minutes before cooking. They are sold in two-ounce packages and up.

BIRDS' NESTS or SWALLOWS' NESTS　燕窩

These special nests made by Asian swifts are used in a rare Chinese delicacy, **Birds' Nest Soup.** The birds' nests are actually a gelatinous substance which softens upon soaking. They are sold by weight in gift boxes.

BLACK BEANS, SALTED or FERMENTED　豆豉

Salted black beans are used as a seasoning. They have a strong flavor and are always used with fresh garlic. The beans are sold in plastic bags. Refrigerated in a covered container, they will keep indefinitely.

BOK CHOY　白菜

Bok choy has smooth, thick, white stems 12 to 16 inches long with dark green leaves. Use both stems and leaves. Stored in the refrigerator in a plastic bag, it will keep for three to four days.

CABBAGE, CHINESE　黄芽白菜

Chinese cabbage has flat stems 2 to 4 inches wide. Its pale yellow to light green leaves are tightly packed. Use both the stems and leaves. Stored in the refrigerator in a plastic bag, it will keep for about a week.

CHILI PEPPER, DRIED RED　乾辣椒

Chili pepper is an extremely hot seasoning used in Szechwan and Hunan dishes. It is packaged either whole (about two inches long) or crushed.

CILANTRO or CHINESE PARSLEY　香菜

Cilantro, also called Chinese parsley, is an aromatic herb with flat leaves. It is used for both seasoning and garnishing. Cut off the roots, rinse in a large pot of cold water, and drain well. Refrigerate in a plastic bag or covered container. It will keep for about a week.

CLOUD EAR, BLACK　雲耳

Black cloud ear is a dried fungus, thin and brittle. Used mainly for extra texture, cloud ear does not have any particular flavor. It is sold in plastic packages and will keep in a covered container at room temperature for months.

COOKING OIL　油

In Chinese cooking, use flavorless vegetable oils such as corn oil, cottonseed oil, peanut oil, soybean oil, or sunflower oil. My choice is Mazola corn oil. Vegetable oil can tolerate the high heat needed for stir-frying. Since it is flavorless, it will not mask the ingredients. Butter or margarine should never be used in Chinese cooking. When the Chinese started cooking with vegetable oil centuries ago, they certainly had no idea that vegetable oil was better for their health than animal fat.

COOKING WINE　酒

Chinese cooks use rice wine for marinating and cooking. Since it is not readily available in the United States, Gallo Dry Sherry is a good substitute.

CORNSTARCH 玉蜀黍粉（玉米粉）

Cornstarch is not a Chinese ingredient, but it is extensively used in Chinese cooking. Cornstarch serves two purposes in Chinese cooking: (1) It helps to tenderize meat by sealing in juices when the marinated meat hits the hot oil. (2) It makes a smooth, thickening sauce. Unlike flour, cornstarch is clear when cooked, so it will not mask the color of the food. Always mix cornstarch thoroughly with cold water or other liquid before adding to the wok; otherwise you will have a lumpy sauce.

DATES, DRIED RED 紅棗

Dried red dates have puckered skin and are primarily used in dessert recipes. They are sold in plastic packages and will keep in a covered container in the refrigerator for months.

DATES, PRESERVED BLACK 黑棗

Black dates are also used in dessert recipes. They are sold in plastic packages or boxes. Most preserved black dates are pitted. They will keep in a covered container in the refrigerator for months.

EGG ROLL WRAPPERS 春捲皮

Made of flour, water, salt, and eggs, fresh or frozen wrappers (each about 6½ x 6½ inches) come in packages weighing about a pound. If tightly wrapped, they will keep for a week in the refrigerator or for months in the freezer.

FIVE-SPICE POWDER 五香粉

Five-spice powder is a combination of five ground spices: anise, Szechwan pepper, fennel, cinnamon, and cloves. It is sold in a plastic bag. After opening, transfer to a tightly covered container.

GINGER POWDER, SPICED 薑粉

Spiced ginger powder is not ordinary ginger powder, but a combination of ginger powder and other spices. It is a very special condiment used in the dipping sauce for **White-Cut Chicken**. (Do not substitute regular powdered ginger.)

36

GINGER ROOT　　生 薑

A sandy-colored knobby herb, ginger root should be smooth and firm when fresh. It can be stored in the refrigerator vegetable drawer for two to three weeks. To keep the ginger root longer, peel, slice, and refrigerate in a covered glass jar filled with dry sherry or rice wine.

GINGKO NUTS or WHITE NUTS　　白 果

Gingko nuts are used mostly in desserts and savory stuffing. They are available in cans. After opening, refrigerate in a covered container filled with tap water, change the water daily. They will keep for a week.

HOISIN SAUCE　　海 鮮 醬

Hoisin sauce is creamy and brownish red. It is made from soybeans, flour, sugar, vinegar, fermented rice, chili, and other spices, and sold in one-pound cans. After opening, transfer to a covered container. It keeps in the refrigerator for months.

HOT PEPPER, FRESH　　辣 椒

When the recipe asks for fresh hot peppers, use chilies serranos or jalapeños.

LONGAN PULP, PRESERVED　　龍 眼 肉

Longan pulp is used in Chinese desserts, such as **Eight-Treasure Rice Pudding**. It is dark brown and sweet. It is sold in plastic packages and should be refrigerated in a covered container. It keeps for months.

LOTUS SEEDS, DRIED　　蓮 子

Dried lotus seeds are used in desserts, savory stuffing, or soup. The brown skin is edible, but you can also buy them blanched. They are sold by weight in plastic packages. Soak in hot water for 30 minutes before using. Dried lotus seeds keep for months in a covered container in the refrigerator.

MUSHROOMS, CHINESE DRIED　　冬 菇

Chinese dried mushrooms are used both for their unique flavor and for their texture. The size ranges from 1 inch to 3 inches; the bigger, thicker ones are more expensive. They are sold in plastic packages. If refrigerated, they will keep indefinitely.

MUSHROOMS, STRAW　　草 菇

Straw mushrooms are available in cans; they look like miniature umbrellas. After opening, refrigerate in a covered container filled with tap water and change the water daily. They will keep for about four or five days.

MUSTARD POWDER   芥　末

Mustard is served as a dip for Deep-Fried Wontons, Egg Rolls, or any dish. The powder is sold by weight in tin cans or plastic bags. To use, mix with water until creamy.

NOODLES, CHINESE   麵

Because noodles are long, they are a symbol of longevity. The Chinese serve noodles on birthdays as Americans would serve birthday cakes. They come fresh or dried. Most noodles are made of flour and water; some contain eggs. If Chinese noodles are unavailable, use vermicelli.

OYSTER SAUCE   蠔　油

Made from oyster extract, water, salt, cornstarch, and caramel, oyster sauce is a thick brown sauce. It is sold in bottles or large cans. It is used in both cooking and dipping. It will keep for months at room temperature, and will keep longer if refrigerated.

PLUM SAUCE   蘇　梅　醬

Used as is for dipping or combined with other ingredients, plum sauce is made of plum pulp, sugar, vinegar, salt, ginger, chili, and garlic. It is sold in 16-ounce cans. After opening, refrigerate in a covered container. It will keep for months.

RICE, SWEET or GLUTINOUS   糯　米

Sweet rice is used for desserts or savory stuffing. It is sold by weight in bags.

SEAWEED, PURPLE, or LAVER   紫　菜

Purple seaweed, also called laver, looks like a piece of thin, dark, purple paper. The dried seaweed is pressed into sheets and wrapped in plastic packages.

SESAME OIL 蔴 油

Sesame oil, made from roasted sesame seeds, is used for seasoning usually at the end of cooking, or as dressing for Chinese salads. (Do not confuse the Chinese version with the cold pressed sesame oil sold in American supermarkets.) It keeps for months at room temperature, and will keep longer if refrigerated.

SESAME SEED PASTE 芝 蔴 醬

Sesame seed paste has a very strong aroma. It is used primarily as a salad dressing. It comes covered with oil in a jar and will keep in the refrigerator for several months. Peanut butter is a good substitute.

SHRIMP, DRIED 蝦 米

Dried shrimp are used in small quantities for seasoning. Sold by weight in plastic packages, they are bright orange-pink. Store in a covered container in the refrigerator. They will keep for a couple of months. Soak in warm water for 10 minutes before using.

SNOW PEAS 雪 豆

Snow peas are flat and green. Fresh snow peas should be crisp, not limp. Refrigerate in a plastic bag. They will keep for about a week. Frozen snow peas should be avoided because they are soggy.

SOY SAUCE 醬 油

Indispensable in Chinese cooking, soy sauce is made from soybeans, wheat, yeast, sugar, salt, and plenty of sunshine. It is sold in bottles or large cans. Soy sauce comes in a wide range of flavors and shades, from light to dark. As a rule, light soy sauce is used with chicken and seafood while the dark kind is used with beef and pork. To make the recipes less complicated without sacrificing taste and color, all recipes in this book were kitchen-tested with one medium soy sauce, Kikkoman brand. The amount of soy sauce used in the recipes will vary depending upon the flavor and color required.

STAR ANISE 八 角

Whole star anise looks like an eight-pointed star about one inch across. It is sold by weight in plastic packages and keeps indefinitely in a tightly covered container.

SUGAR, ROCK 冰 糖

Rock sugar comes in chunks that look like crystals. It has a subtle taste and is used in most braised or "red-cooked" dishes. Sold in one-pound plastic packages, it keeps indefinitely.

SZECHWAN PEPPERCORNS or CHINESE PEPPERCORNS　花椒

Used in regional cuisine, these peppercorns are a product of the Szechwan Province. They are sold by weight in bags and keep indefinitely in a covered container.

TIGER LILY BUDS, DRIED　金針

Dried tiger lily buds are dark gold in color, about 3 to 4 inches long. They are sold in packages in Chinese specialty stores and will keep for months. Before cooking, soak in hot water for about 10 minutes. Snap off the hard ends, rinse, and cut in half.

WATER CHESTNUTS　荸薺

Fresh water chestnuts are bulb-like, about one inch across with russet skins. Fresh ones are not readily available, but canned ones are a good substitute. After opening, cover the water chestnuts with tap water. Store in the refrigerator up to a week, changing the water daily.

WINTER MELON　冬瓜

Winter melon is shaped like a watermelon; however, it has a powdery, green rind. It weighs from 10 to 30 pounds. You can grow them in your back yard. Winter melons are also sold by weight in some Chinese specialty stores. A whole one will keep for months in a cool place. After cutting open, cover with plastic wrap and refrigerate. It will keep for about a week.

WONTON WRAPPERS　餛飩皮

Made of flour, water, salt, and eggs, wonton wrappers are sold fresh or frozen in packages of 12 or more ounces. The dough is cut into 3¼ x 3¼-inch squares. If tightly wrapped, they will keep for a week in the refrigerator or for months in the freezer.

CUTTING TECHNIQUES

If there is one thing that makes Chinese cooking different from other cuisines, it is the way foods are cut before cooking. As a rule, all the ingredients in a recipe, whether meat or vegetable, should be about the same size to ensure uniform cooking. Cutting food into bite-sized pieces saves cooking time and energy and also preserves nutrients because the food does not get overcooked.

The following definitions are only guidelines. You certainly do not need to measure each piece you cut.

SLICE: Slice food into pieces about 1½ to 2 inches long; ¾ to 1 inch wide; and ⅛ to ¼ inch thick. Meat should be sliced across the grain, unless otherwise specified in the recipe.

SHRED: Slice food as described above; then cut into shreds 1½ to 2 inches long and ⅛ to ¼ inch thick and wide. The shreds should be about the size of toothpicks.

MINCE: Starting with shreds, as described above, cut ingredients into 1/16- to ⅛-inch pieces.

DICE: Cut ingredients into ¼- to ½-inch cubes.

CUBE: Cut ingredients into ¾- to 1-inch cubes.

CHOP FINELY: Cut ingredients into ⅛- to ¼-inch pieces.

CUT DIAGONALLY: Cut on the diagonal to expose more surface. This is a common cutting technique for vegetables.

ROLL-CUT: This technique is used with long, stick-like vegetables, such as asparagus and carrots. Cut vegetable diagonally about 1 inch long. Roll vegetable 90° away from you and cut diagonally again. Repeat until you have cut up the whole vegetable.

SMASH: This method eliminates the hard work of peeling garlic cloves. Strike the clove with the flat side of a cleaver blade. The skin will break and you can peel it very easily.

COOKING METHODS

Most Chinese dishes are simple, even for beginners. You can easily prepare a variety of recipes once you master the cooking techniques.

STIR-FRYING, the technique most associated with Chinese wok cooking, is cooking bite-sized pieces of food in a small amount of oil over intense heat while tossing and stirring briskly. Although stir-frying is a very simple cooking method, there are some rules you must observe to make the dish successful.

1. All preparations must be completed before cooking starts. Every ingredient should be cut as required in the recipe. Meat should be marinated, and all sauce ingredients should be combined in a small bowl.

2. Preheat the wok* over high heat, then add the oil and swirl to coat the lower portion of the wok with oil. When oil is hot, start adding ingredients in the order given in the recipe.

3. For timing, follow the guidelines given in the recipe and also use your own judgement. Many factors influence cooking time: heat source (gas or electric range); size of heating coils on electric ranges; weight of the wok; distance between the wok base and the heat source; thickness of the ingredients; amount of water left on drained ingredients.

PAN-FRYING is browning food by searing in a small amount of oil without turning. It is best done in a non-stick skillet over low to medium heat. In Chinese cooking, pan-frying is used to cook dumplings, fish, and noodles.

DEEP-FRYING is cooking food in a large amount of hot oil at 375°F. The oil can be reused. Cool it to room temperature, cover, and refrigerate. If a residue remains, strain the oil before storing. You can freshen the oil by adding a couple of slices of ginger root to the hot oil. When the ginger root slices turn brown, discard them; then add food. This is especially useful if you have deep-fried seafood before.

STEAMING, or cooking with moist heat, is a very clean and healthy cooking method because little or no oil is used. The Chinese steam pastries, seafood, meat, and poultry, but seldom vegetables. For recipes that call for steaming, use a Chinese steamer or improvise one (see page15).When steaming food, observe these rules:

* Only for traditional woks made of cast iron or carbon steel.

1. Water should be brought to a brisk boil before adding the food and kept at the boiling point during cooking.

2. The water line should be at least one inch below the lowest tier or rack, so the water will not bubble into the food. Replenish with additional boiling water as needed during cooking.

3. Most foods should be placed on a heat-proof dish in the steamer. (Pastry should be placed directly on the tiers of the steamer.) The dish should be smaller than the steamer, so the steam can circulate freely.

BRAISING or "RED-COOKING" is cooking food in large amounts of soy sauce over low heat. The soy sauce gives the finished product a reddish-brown sheen, hence it is called "red-cooking". It is a popular method of cooking fish, poultry, or meat.

ROASTING is cooking strips of meat or whole poultry on a rack. Although ovens are not a standard appliance in Chinese kitchens, this book is written for the American kitchen and includes roasting recipes.

SMOKING is actually a way of flavoring rather than cooking. The meat or poultry is cured with salt and pepper overnight in the refrigerator, then steam cooked, and finally smoked. Sugar is the main smoking agent. When heat is applied, sugar burns, creating the smoke.

MEASUREMENTS

The following measurements are used throughout this book. All recipes list dry ingredients before liquids, so you do not have to dry the measuring spoons between measurements.

LIQUID AND VOLUME EQUIVALENTS

Dash (a few grains)	= less than ⅛ teaspoon
1 teaspoon	= ⅓ tablespoon
1 tablespoon	= 3 teaspoons
4 tablespoons	= ¼ cup
5 tablespoons + 1 teaspoon	= ⅓ cup
8 tablespoons	= ½ cup
16 tablespoons	= 1 cup or 8 ounces
2 cups	= 1 pint
1 quart	= 2 pints
1 gallon	= 4 quarts

WEIGHT EQUIVALENTS

¼ pound	= 4 ounces
½ pound	= 8 ounces
1 pound	= 16 ounces

Hors d'Oeuvres

Barbecued Spareribs (Serves 6 to 10)　　烤　排　骨

3 pounds pork spareribs*

Marinade:
3 cloves garlic, finely minced
1 teaspoon salt
1 teaspoon lemon juice
1 tablespoon oil
1 tablespoon honey
2 tablespoons dry sherry
3 tablespoons hoisin sauce
　or Chinese barbecue sauce
3 tablespoons soy sauce

To Prepare Ahead:

1. Trim fat off ribs.

2. Mix the marinade ingredients in a long pan and dip each rib strip in the marinade, coating well on both sides.

3. Marinate the ribs for at least 4 hours or overnight in the refrigerator.

To Cook:

1. Place the ribs on a barbecue grill over medium heat. Barbecue for about 30 minutes, turning the ribs 2 or 3 times while cooking.

2. Check for doneness by cutting into a thick piece of the meat; there should be no pink color remaining.

3. With a cleaver or sharp knife, separate the individual ribs by cutting between the bones. Serve as is or with plum sauce.

Tip • Spareribs can also be cooked in the oven. Preheat the oven to 375°F. Line the roasting pan with foil and add some water to prevent smoking. Put the pan on the lower rack. Lay the marinaded ribs on the upper rack and roast for 30 minutes. Separate the individual ribs by cutting between the bones.

* Ask the butcher to cut the ribs across the bones into 1½-inch strips.

Deep-Fried Shrimp Balls (Yields 2 dozen) 炸 蝦 球

       1 pound small shrimp in shells
       2 teaspoons chopped ginger root
       3 ounces ground pork
       ⅛ teaspoon freshly ground pepper
       1 teaspoon salt
       2 tablespoons cornstarch
       1 teaspoon dry sherry
       ½ teaspoon lemon juice
       1 egg white, beaten until foamy
       3 cups oil for deep-frying

To Prepare Ahead:

1. Shell, devein, and rinse shrimp; drain thoroughly.

2. With a cleaver, chop shrimp very finely into a pulplike mass.

3. In a small bowl, combine 2 tablespoons water with chopped ginger root. Press the ginger with the back of a teaspoon to release the flavor and let stand in the liquid for 10 minutes; strain, discarding ginger root.

4. Combine all ingredients except oil. Stir in a circular motion until a smooth paste forms (about 3 minutes).

To Cook:

1. Heat 3 cups oil in a wok over high heat to 375°F.

2. Shape shrimp mixture into 1-inch balls and drop into the hot oil, one at a time. Deep-fry for 3 to 5 minutes.

3. Drain on paper towels. Serve with roasted salt-Szechwan pepper (see below).

Tips • Roasted salt-Szechwan pepper: In a small saucepan, combine 1 tablespoon salt and 1 teaspoon Szechwan peppercorns. Cook over medium heat for 2 minutes, stirring occasionally. Let cool, crush with the handle of your cleaver or a mortar and pestle. Shake the mixture through a fine sieve. Store in a small glass jar.

 • Deep-fried shrimp balls can be frozen. Before serving, thaw and reheat in a preheated 350°F. oven for about 8 minutes or in a microwave oven.

Deep-Fried Wontons (Yields about 45)　炸 餛 飩

    1 green onion
    1 paper-thin slice peeled ginger root

Seasoning sauce:
      1 teaspoon cornstarch
      ¼ teaspoon salt
      1 teaspoon sesame oil
      2 teaspoons dry sherry
      2 teaspoons soy sauce
      2 tablespoons water

    1 tablespoon oil
    ½ pound lean ground pork
    12 ounces wonton wrappers
    3 cups oil for deep-frying

To Make Filling:

1. Finely chop green onion.

2. Mince slice of peeled ginger root.

3. Combine seasoning sauce ingredients in a bowl.

4. Heat 1 tablespoon oil in a wok over high heat. Add green onion, ginger root, and pork. Stir-fry until the pork loses its reddish color. Remove excess fat, if any.

5. Add seasoning sauce to wok, stirring constantly until thickened. Remove to a dish and cool to room temperature.

To Assemble:

Have the wonton wrappers, the filling, and a small bowl of water within easy reach.

1. Put about ¾ teaspoon of filling in the center of each wrapper.

2. Fold the wrapper away from you, forming 2 overlapping triangles.

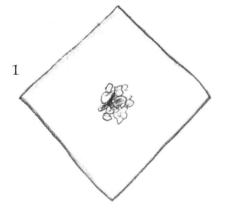

48

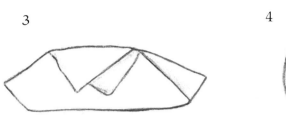

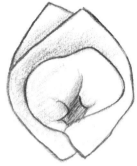

3. Flip the upper points of triangle toward you.

4. Lift the outside corners and bring them together to create a groove around the mound of the filling. With your fingertips, moisten one corner with water and place the other corner on top, pinching together firmly.

To Deep-Fry:

1. Heat 3 cups oil in a wok or deep-fryer over high heat to 375°F. Or you can test the oil by dropping a small piece (about ½-inch square) of wonton wrapper into the hot oil. If it comes to the surface immediately, the oil is hot enough.

2. Carefully add about 10 wontons to the oil; deep-fry for a couple of minutes or until golden brown and crisp.

3. Remove with a strainer or slotted spoon; drain on a serving dish lined with paper towels.

4. Repeat with the remaining wontons.

To Serve:

Serve with hot mustard, and sweet and sour sauce.

Hot mustard:
Mix 2 tablespoons mustard powder with enough water to form a creamy sauce.

Sweet and sour sauce:
Mix 2 tablespoons sugar, 2 tablespoons catsup, 3 tablespoons plum sauce, and 3 tablespoons white vinegar.

Tips   • Wontons can be frozen after being assembled. Thaw completely before deep-frying. You can also deep-fry them first and then freeze.

• Deep-fried wontons can be kept warm in an oven at 200°F. for 30 minutes or reheated at 425°F. for 3 to 5 minutes; if frozen, 6 to 7 minutes.

• Ground beef can be substituted for the ground pork.

Deep-Fried Shrimp Toast (Yields 20 pieces)　　蝦 吐 司

¾ pound small shrimp in shells

Marinade for shrimp:
　　1 egg white, beaten until foamy
　　½ teaspoon salt
　　2 tablespoons cornstarch
　　1 teaspoon dry sherry

2 water chestnuts
5 slices day-old white bread
3 cups oil for deep-frying

To Prepare Ahead:

1. Shell, devein, and rinse shrimp; drain thoroughly.

2. With a cleaver, chop shrimp very finely into a pulplike mass. Place in a mixing bowl.

3. Add the marinade ingredients to the shrimp. Stir in a circular motion until smooth.

4. Finely mince the water chestnuts and add to the shrimp mixture.

5. Trim the crust off the bread slices and cut each slice into quarters.

6. Spread about 1 tablespoon of the shrimp mixture on each bread square, mounding slightly.

To Cook:

1. Heat 3 cups oil in a wok over high heat to 350° F. Drop in bread squares, shrimp side down, about 10 at a time. Fry for 1 minute; turn over and fry for another 30 seconds. Then turn over again and fry for 30 seconds more.

2. Drain the shrimp toast in a dish lined with paper towels.

3. Deep-fry the remainder and serve as an hors d'oeuvre.

Tip　• Shrimp toast can be frozen and reheated. Fry as directed in the recipe; cool to room temperature before freezing. To reheat, place in a preheated 350°F. oven for 5 to 8 minutes.

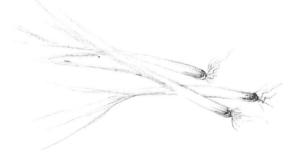

Egg Rolls (Yields 15)　春 捲

　　½ pound lean pork*

　　Marinade for pork:
　　　1 teaspoon cornstarch
　　　2 teaspoons dry sherry
　　　1 tablespoon soy sauce

　　½ pound small shrimp in shells
　　1½ teaspoons salt
　　3 Chinese dried mushrooms
　　½ pound fresh mung bean sprouts
　　4 stalks celery
　　2 green onions

　　Sauce:
　　　½ teaspoon sugar
　　　1 teaspoon cornstarch
　　　1 tablespoon water
　　　1 tablespoon soy sauce

　　5 tablespoons oil
　　15 egg roll wrappers (about 1 pound)
　　4 cups oil for deep-frying

To Prepare Ahead:

1. Shred the pork by slicing it thinly across the grain, then cutting the slices into strips (⅛ x ⅛ x 2 inches). Add the marinade ingredients to the meat and toss to coat thoroughly; let stand for 30 minutes or longer.

2. Shell, devein, and cut shrimp into small strips lengthwise. Add ½ teaspoon salt to the shrimp and mix well.

3. Soak the dried mushrooms in a cup of hot water until soft, about 20 minutes. Rinse, squeeze dry, and cut off the stems. Slice the caps thinly. Set aside with the shrimp.

4. Rinse bean sprouts in a pot of cold water and drain well.

5. Shred celery and green onions.

6. Combine sauce ingredients in a small bowl.

To Make Filling:

1. Heat 2 tablespoons oil in a wok over high heat. Add bean sprouts, celery, and 1 teaspoon salt; stir-fry for 1 to 2 minutes. Transfer to a colander to drain.

---

* Use boneless pork roast, butterfly pork chops or pork tenderloin.

2. Wipe the wok dry and add 3 tablespoons oil. When hot, add green onions and pork; stir-fry for 2 minutes.

3. Add shrimp and mushrooms; stir-fry until the shrimp turn pink.

4. Return the vegetables to the wok; add sauce, stirring for a few seconds. Remove to a colander and cool to room temperature.

To Assemble:

Have the egg roll wrappers, the filling, and a small bowl of water within easy reach.

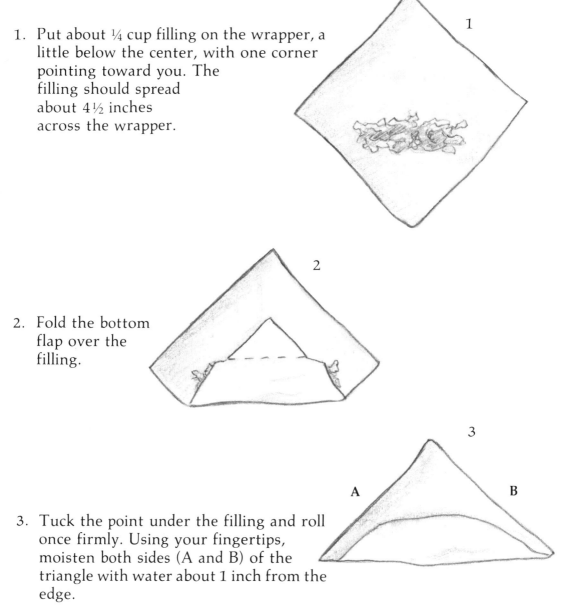

1. Put about ¼ cup filling on the wrapper, a little below the center, with one corner pointing toward you. The filling should spread about 4½ inches across the wrapper.

2. Fold the bottom flap over the filling.

3. Tuck the point under the filling and roll once firmly. Using your fingertips, moisten both sides (A and B) of the triangle with water about 1 inch from the edge.

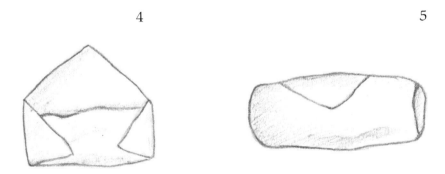

4. Fold the right and left flaps toward center. Moisten both flaps and the triangular surface with water again.

5. Roll firmly all the way, making sure the edges seal well.

6. Place egg rolls on a tray in a single layer; do not stack.

To Deep-Fry:

1. Heat 4 cups oil in a wok or deep-fryer over high heat to 375°F. Or you can test the oil by dropping a small piece (about ½-inch square) of wrapper into the hot oil. If it comes to the surface at once, the oil is hot enough.

2. Slide 5 egg rolls into the oil and deep-fry for about 3 to 5 minutes or until golden brown, turning 2 or 3 times.

3. Remove and drain on paper towels.

4. Deep-fry the remaining egg rolls in two more batches.

To Serve:

Serve with hot mustard (page 49) and sweet and sour sauce (page 49).

Tip • Egg rolls must be deep-fried immediately after wrapping. If you want to prepare them in advance, deep-fry until slightly brown. Drain, cool, and refrigerate or freeze. To reheat, preheat oven to 425°F. Put egg rolls directly on the middle rack; bake for 8 minutes if cold, or 12 minutes if frozen.

Egg Rolls with Shredded Chicken (Yields 15)　　鷄絲春捲

　　1 pound chicken breast, boned and skinned*

Marinade for chicken:
　　½ teaspoon salt
　　2 teaspoons cornstarch
　　2 teaspoons dry sherry
　　2 teaspoons soy sauce
　　1 tablespoon water

½ pound fresh mung bean sprouts
4 stalks celery
2 green onions

Sauce:
　　½ teaspoon sugar
　　1 teaspoon cornstarch
　　1 tablespoon soy sauce
　　1 tablespoon water

5 tablespoons oil
1 teaspoon salt
15 egg roll wrappers (about 1 pound)
4 cups oil for deep-frying

To Prepare Ahead:

1. Shred the chicken by slicing it thinly across the grain, then cutting the slices into strips (⅛ x ⅛ x 2 inches). Add the marinade ingredients and toss to coat thoroughly; let stand for 30 minutes or longer.

2. Rinse bean sprouts in a pot of cold water and drain well.

3. Shred celery and green onions.

4. Combine sauce ingredients in a small bowl.

To Make Filling:

1. Heat 2 tablespoons oil in a wok over high heat. Add bean sprouts, celery, and 1 teaspoon salt; stir-fry for 1 to 2 minutes. Transfer to a colander to drain.

2. Wipe the wok dry and add 3 tablespoons oil. When hot, add green onions and chicken. Stir-fry for 3 to 4 minutes or until chicken turns white.

3. Return vegetables to the wok; add sauce, stirring for a few seconds. Remove to a colander and cool to room temperature.

To Assemble, Deep-fry, and Serve:

See recipe for **Egg Rolls** (pages 52 and 53).

---

* See directions on page 115. You need almost 2 pounds of chicken breast with bone and skin to get 1 pound of meat.

Sweet and Sour Spareribs (Serves 5 to 8) 糖醋排骨

2½ pounds pork spareribs*

Marinade for spareribs:
  1 teaspoon salt
  1 teaspoon sugar
  1 tablespoon soy sauce
  1 tablespoon dry sherry

Sweet and sour sauce:
  2 tablespoons sugar
  1 teaspoon cornstarch
  1 tablespoon water
  1 tablespoon soy sauce
  2 tablespoons white vinegar
  2 tablespoons catsup
  ½ teaspoon sesame oil

3 cups oil for deep-frying

To Prepare Ahead:

1. With a cleaver or knife, trim off excess fat from ribs. Separate the ribs by cutting between the bones.

2. Put the spareribs in a large mixing bowl. Add the marinade and toss to coat evenly; let stand for 30 minutes or longer.

3. In a 4-quart saucepan, combine the sauce ingredients; set aside.

To Cook:

1. Heat 3 cups oil in a wok over high heat to 350°F. Add ⅓ of the spareribs to the hot oil and deep-fry for 5 minutes or until fully cooked; drain on a serving dish lined with paper towels.

2. Deep-fry the remaining ribs in two more batches.

3. Bring sauce ingredients to a boil over high heat, stirring constantly. Add the deep-fried ribs to the saucepan, mix thoroughly and cook until the liquid is absorbed. Serve hot or at room temperature.

Tip • You can cook this dish a day ahead, cool, cover, and refrigerate. Bring the ribs to room temperature or reheat in a microwave oven before serving.

---

* Ask the butcher to cut the ribs across the bones into 1½-inch strips.

Soups and Fire Pot

Chicken Broth (Serves 6 to 8)　　鷄　湯

    1 (4-pound) chicken
    2 green onions, cut into 3-inch pieces
    8 cups water
    1 slice peeled ginger root
    Salt to taste

1. Rinse chicken and remove fat from the cavity.

2. In a 6-quart heavy saucepan, combine all ingredients except salt and bring to a boil over high heat.

3. Reduce heat to medium-low; simmer for 1½ hours. Add salt to taste.

4. Remove chicken, skim off fat and strain broth through a fine sieve. The broth is ready to be used in soup or other cooking.

Tips • You can also use a slow cooker.

- To remove fat easily, chill broth and lift off congealed fat. Reheat and serve.

- Fresh broth can only be stored in the refrigerator for a day. To keep it longer, freeze it.

Egg Drop Soup (Serves 2 to 3)　　蛋　花　湯

    1 egg
    1 tablespoon cornstarch
    2½ cups chicken broth (see preceding recipe)
    1 green onion, chopped
    Dash white pepper
    Salt to taste

To Prepare Ahead:

1. Beat egg lightly.

2. Combine cornstarch with 2 tablespoons water.

To Cook:

1. In a 3-quart saucepan, bring chicken broth to a boil over high heat.

2. Give cornstarch mixture a quick stir to blend it and add to the broth. Stir for a few seconds until the broth boils.

3. Slowly add egg and gently stir once; remove from heat immediately.

4. Sprinkle with chopped green onion, white pepper, and salt to taste. Serve at once.

Seaweed Egg Drop Soup (Serves 2 to 3)　紫菜蛋花湯

     1 egg
     1 tablespoon cornstarch
     2½ cups chicken broth (page 57)
     1 sheet purple seaweed (laver)
     1 green onion, chopped
     Dash white pepper
     Salt to taste

To Prepare Ahead:

1. Beat egg lightly.

2. Combine cornstarch with 2 tablespoons water.

To Cook:

1. In a 3-quart saucepan, bring chicken broth to a boil over high heat.

2. Reduce heat to low, add seaweed, and simmer for 3 minutes. Stir to break up the seaweed.

3. Return heat to high, give cornstarch a quick stir to blend it, and add to the broth. Stir for a few seconds until the broth boils.

4. Slowly add egg and gently stir once; remove from heat immediately.

5. Sprinkle with chopped green onion, white pepper, and salt to taste. Serve at once.

Tomato Egg Drop Soup (Serves 2 to 3)　蕃茄蛋花湯

     1 tomato
     1 egg
     2½ cups chicken broth (page 57)
     1 green onion, chopped
     Dash white pepper
     Salt to taste

To Prepare Ahead:

1. Cut tomato into 12 wedges.

2. Beat egg lightly.

To Cook:

1. In a 3-quart saucepan, bring chicken broth to a boil over high heat.

2. Add tomato and cook for 1 minute.

3. Slowly add egg and gently stir once; remove from heat immediately.

4. Sprinkle with chopped green onion, white pepper, and salt to taste. Serve at once.

Chicken and Dried Mushroom Soup (Serves 6 to 8)　冬菇鷄湯

　　　　1 (3- to 4-pound) chicken
　　　　2 green onions, cut into 3-inch pieces
　　　　6 to 8 cups water
　　　　1 slice peeled ginger root
　　　　10 Chinese dried mushrooms
　　　　Salt to taste

1. Rinse the chicken and remove fat from the cavity.

2. Place all ingredients, except mushrooms and salt, in a 4- to 6-quart saucepan and bring to a boil over high heat. Reduce heat to low and simmer for 1 hour.

3. While simmering the chicken, soak mushrooms in a cup of hot water until soft, about 20 minutes. Rinse and cut off stems.

4. Add mushrooms to the broth; simmer 30 minutes more. Discard the ginger root.

5. Skim off fat and add salt to taste. Serve hot.

Pork and Cellophane Noodle Soup (Serves 4 to 6)　肉片粉絲湯

　　　　1 pound lean pork*
　　　　2 ounces cellophane noodles
　　　　1 pound Chinese cabbage
　　　　5 cups water
　　　　1 slice peeled ginger root
　　　　Salt and pepper to taste

To Prepare Ahead:

1. Slice pork into 1 x 1½-inch slices, ¼ inch thick.

2. Soak cellophane noodles in 4 cups hot water for 10 minutes; discard the water.

3. Rinse and cut Chinese cabbage crosswise into 1-inch pieces.

To Cook:

1. In a 4-quart saucepan, combine pork, water, and ginger root; bring to a boil over high heat. Turn heat to medium-low, cover and simmer for 1 hour. Discard the ginger root.

2. Add Chinese cabbage and cellophane noodles, and cook over medium heat for 8 minutes. Add salt and pepper to taste. Serve hot.

* Use pork roast, pork chops, or pork tenderloin.

Hot and Sour Soup (Serves 6)　　酸 辣 湯

¼ pound boneless lean pork*

Marinade for pork:
1 teaspoon cornstarch
1 teaspoon dry sherry
2 teaspoons soy sauce

4 Chinese dried mushrooms
2 tablespoons dried black cloud ears
1 square fresh, firm bean curd
3 tablespoons cornstarch
1 quart chicken broth (page 57)
½ cup shredded bamboo shoots
1 egg, lightly beaten
2 teaspoons sesame oil
3 tablespoons white vinegar
1 tablespoon soy sauce
1 tablespoon chopped green onion
½ teaspoon white pepper

To Prepare Ahead:

1. Shred the pork by slicing it thinly across the grain, then cutting the slices into tiny strips (⅛ x ⅛ x 2 inches). Add marinade ingredients to the meat and mix thoroughly; let stand for 30 minutes.

2. Soak mushrooms and cloud ears in 2 cups hot water for 20 minutes. Rinse until water is clear. Cut off and discard the stems. Shred the caps into thin strips.

3. Drain bean curd and cut into ¼ x ¼ x 3-inch strips.

4. Mix 3 tablespoons cornstarch with 3 tablespoons water.

To Cook:

1. In a 4-quart saucepan, bring broth to a boil over high heat. Add pork, mushrooms, black cloud ears, and bamboo shoots. Bring to boil; reduce heat to low. Cover and simmer for 3 minutes.

2. Return heat to high. Add bean curd and cornstarch mixture; stir gently until it boils.

3. Slowly add beaten egg, stirring gently once; immediately remove from heat.

4. Add sesame oil, white vinegar, 1 tablespoon soy sauce, and green onion. Sprinkle with white pepper, mix well, and serve. Add more white pepper and vinegar if needed.

* Use butterfly pork chops or pork tenderloin.

Sparerib and Watercress Soup (Serves 4)   西洋菜排骨湯

　　　1 pound pork spareribs*
　　　1 bunch watercress (about 6 ounces)
　　　4 cups water
　　　2 slices peeled ginger root
　　　Salt and pepper to taste

To Prepare Ahead:

1. Separate the ribs between bones and trim off excess fat.

2. Rinse watercress in a large pot of cold water; drain and snap each stem into 2 or 3 pieces.

To Cook:

1. In a 4-quart saucepan, combine ribs, water, and ginger root; cover and bring to a boil over high heat.

2. Turn heat to low and simmer for 1½ hours. Skim off fat and remove ginger root.

3. Return heat to high; add watercress. Bring to a boil, and cook 1 minute more. Add salt and pepper to taste and serve.

Winter Melon Soup (Serves 4)   冬　瓜　湯

　　　2 pounds winter melon
　　　2 ounces Virginia ham *or* other ham
　　　4 cups chicken broth (page 57)
　　　Salt to taste

To Prepare Ahead:

1. Cut off the melon rind; remove seeds and stringy fibers. Cut into 1x1½-inch slices, ¼ inch thick.

2. Cut ham into 1-inch squares, ⅛ inch thick.

To Cook:

1. In a 4-quart saucepan, combine winter melon, ham, and broth; bring to a boil over high heat.

2. Reduce heat to low, cover, and simmer for 10 minutes. Add salt to taste and serve.

Tip　•　For variation you can add several Chinese dried mushrooms (soak for 20 minutes and cut off stems) to the broth with melon. The mushrooms will give a distinct flavor to the soup.

* Ask the butcher to cut the ribs across the bones into 1½-inch strips.

Wonton Soup (Serves 6 to 10) 餛 飩 湯

½ pound lean ground pork

Meat seasonings:

    1 green onion, finely chopped
    1 paper-thin slice peeled ginger root, minced
    ¼ teaspoon salt
    2 teaspoons cornstarch
    1 teaspoon sesame oil
    2 teaspoons dry sherry
    1 tablespoon soy sauce
    2 tablespoons water

4 ounces fresh spinach
   or watercress
12 ounces wonton wrappers (about 45 pieces)
2½ quarts chicken broth (page 57)
1 teaspoon sesame oil
⅛ teaspoon white pepper

To Prepare Ahead:

1. In a small mixing bowl, combine meat with meat seasonings; mix until smooth.

2. Wash spinach or watercress in a pot of cold water; drain and tear into 1½-inch pieces.

To Assemble:

Have the wonton wrappers, the filling, and a small bowl of water within easy reach.

1. Put about ¾ teaspoon filling on the wonton wrapper as shown below.

2. Fold the bottom of the wrapper over the filling and roll.

1

2

3. Roll up, leaving ½ inch border at upper edge.

4. Lift the ends and bring them together. With your fingertips, moisten one end with water and place the other end on top, pinching together firmly.

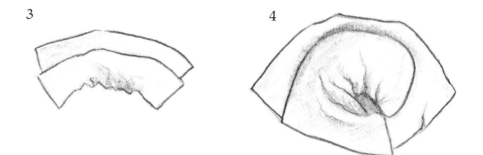

To Cook:

1. In a 6-quart saucepan, bring the broth to a boil over high heat. Drop in wontons, stirring gently once with a ladle.

2. Cover and return to a boil; reduce heat to medium and cook uncovered for 5 minutes.

3. Turn heat to high and add spinach or watercress. Return to a boil, add 1 teaspoon sesame oil, and sprinkle with white pepper. Adjust seasoning and serve at once. (See picture on page 17.)

Tips • Wontons can be frozen after being assembled. Thaw completely and cook as directed.

• Cook enough wontons for one meal (4 to 5 wontons per cup of broth) and freeze the rest.

• Ground beef can be substituted for the pork.

• For another variation, use ¼ pound lean ground pork and ¼ pound minced raw shrimp instead of ½ pound pork.

• Add several slices of Chinese barbecued pork (page 98) to the soup, if desired.

Birds' Nest Soup (Serves 10 to 12)　燕 窩 湯

　　　1 cup dried birds' nests
　　　2 slices peeled ginger root
　　　1 whole chicken breast, boned and skinned*

　　　Marinade for chicken:
　　　　½ teaspoon salt
　　　　1 teaspoon cornstarch
　　　　1 teaspoon dry sherry
　　　　¼ cup water

　　　2 egg whites
　　　4 tablespoons cornstarch
　　　1½ quarts chicken broth (page 57)
　　　Dash white pepper
　　　3 tablespoons minced cooked Virginia ham
　　　or other cooked ham

To Prepare Ahead:

1. Soak the birds' nests in 4 cups hot water for 3 hours. Remove tiny feathers with tweezers; drain and discard water. Cook birds' nests in 4 cups of boiling water with ginger root over medium heat for 10 minutes. Drain the nests; discard water and ginger root.

2. With a cleaver, chop chicken until pasty. Transfer to a mixing bowl. Add marinade ingredients and mix thoroughly.

3. Beat egg whites until frothy and add to the chicken a little at a time, mixing well after each addition.

4. Combine 4 tablespoons cornstarch with 4 tablespoons water.

To Cook:

1. In a 4-quart saucepan, bring chicken broth to a boil over high heat; add the birds' nests. Bring to a boil again, reduce the heat to low, and simmer for 15 minutes.

2. Add cornstarch mixture and chicken, stirring to disperse evenly through the soup.

3. Bring to a boil, and remove from heat immediately; add white pepper. Adjust seasoning, sprinkle the minced ham on top, and serve at once.

* See directions on page 115.

Fire Pot (An eat-as-you-cook meal, serves 6 to 8)   火 鍋

Cook in a Chinese fire pot specially designed for this type of cooking, or use an electric wok or electric skillet.

½ pound lean pork*
½ pound flank steak
½ pound fillet of fresh trout
1 whole chicken breast, boned and skinned**
4 ounces cellophane noodles
½ pound medium shrimp in shells
4 squares firm bean curd
1 pound Chinese cabbage
1 pound fresh spinach
1 head Romaine lettuce
1 (8-ounce) jar small oysters
2 quarts chicken broth (page 57)

Dipping sauce:
    2 tablespoons soy sauce
    2 tablespoons dry sherry
    3 tablespoons oyster sauce
    1 tablespoon sesame oil
    2 teaspoons hot bean sauce (optional)

To Prepare Ahead:

1. Place pork, beef, trout, and chicken breast in the freezer until firm enough for easy slicing. Slice into paper-thin 1 x 2-inch pieces. Arrange each kind of meat attractively in overlapping layers on a separate serving plate.

2. In a large bowl, soak the cellophane noodles in 4 cups of hot water for 10 minutes. Drain and discard the water; cut into 5-inch lengths.

3. Shell and devein shrimp. Arrange each in a butterfly shape on a serving plate.

4. Slice bean curd ¼ inch thick and place on a serving plate.

5. Rinse, drain, and cut Chinese cabbage, spinach, and Romaine lettuce crosswise into 1-inch pieces. Put them separately on a large platter.

6. Strain oysters and transfer to a dish.

7. Mix ingredients for dipping sauce in a bowl, and ladle 1 tablespoon sauce into individual rice bowls.

---

  * Use pork tenderloin, boneless pork roast, or butterfly pork chops.
** See directions on page 115.

To Cook:

1. Bring the chicken broth to a boil in a 3-quart saucepan; pour into the fire pot or electric wok (set at 350°F.). Keep the broth simmering throughout the meal.

2. Using chopsticks, each guest takes some food (meat, seafood, cellophane noodles, bean curd, or vegetables) from the serving plates and transfers it to the simmering broth. When cooked to taste, dip in the sauce and eat.

3. The broth can be served as soup at end of meal.

Tips
- The individual place setting for this meal includes a pair of bamboo or wooden chopsticks (heat-proof), a rice bowl, a soup spoon, and a saucer.

- Fire pot is best served on a cold winter evening when you and your guests have plenty of leisure time.

- The meat and vegetables listed in this recipe are the most popular ones; you can omit some or substitute others.

Bean Curd, Eggs, and Vegetables

Bean Curd with Barbecued Pork (Serves 2)　叉燒豆腐

    4 squares firm bean curd
    ¼ pound barbecued pork (page 98)

Thickening sauce:
    2 teaspoons cornstarch
    1 teaspoon soy sauce
    1 tablespoon oyster sauce
    ½ cup chicken broth

    4 tablespoons oil
    ½ teaspoon salt
    2 green onions, cut into 1½-inch pieces

To Prepare Ahead:

1. Cut each square of bean curd into ½-inch slices.

2. Slice barbecued pork into ¾ x 2-inch slices, ⅛ inch thick.

3. Mix sauce ingredients together in a small bowl.

To Cook:

1. In a large non-stick skillet, heat 3 tablespoons oil over medium-high heat. Carefully place the bean curd slices in the pan in a single layer. Pan-fry for about 2 minutes undisturbed or until golden brown on bottom.

2. Turn the bean curd over and pan-fry until golden brown on the other side. Sprinkle with salt; remove skillet from the heat.

3. Heat 1 tablespoon oil in the wok over high heat. Add green onions and barbecued pork; heat through.

4. Transfer bean curd slices to the wok and add the thickening sauce. Stir gently until thickened and serve. (See picture on pages 20 and 21.)

Bean Curd with Mushrooms (Serves 2)　蘑 菇 豆 腐

    4 squares bean curd
    8 ounces fresh mushrooms

Thickening sauce:
    1 tablespoon cornstarch
    2 tablespoons water
    2 tablespoons oyster sauce
    1 teaspoon sesame oil

    ½ cup chicken broth
    4 tablespoons oil
    1 teaspoon salt
    1 green onion, chopped

To Prepare Ahead:

1. Cut each square of bean curd into ½-inch slices.

2. Rinse, drain, and cut mushrooms into ½-inch slices.

3. Mix sauce ingredients in a small bowl.

To Cook:

1. Heat 4 tablespoons oil in a wok over high heat. Add mushrooms and ½ teaspoon salt; stir-fry for 1 minute and remove to a plate.

2. Add chicken broth to the wok; carefully add bean curd slices and ½ teaspoon salt. Cook over high heat for 2 minutes, stirring gently once or twice.

3. Return mushrooms to the wok and add sauce mixture. Stir carefully until thickened.

4. Transfer to a deep dish and sprinkle with chopped green onion.

Spicy Bean Curd (Serves 2 to 3)　麻婆豆腐

4 squares bean curd

Seasoning sauce:

½ teaspoon salt
1 tablespoon hot bean sauce
1 tablespoon soy sauce
2 tablespoons oyster sauce
⅓ cup chicken broth

2 teaspoons cornstarch
2 tablespoons oil
1 teaspoon chopped garlic
¼ teaspoon minced ginger root
4 ounces lean ground pork
½ teaspoon sesame oil
1 green onion, chopped

To Prepare Ahead:

1. Cut each square of bean curd into 9 equal parts.

2. Mix ingredients for seasoning sauce in a small bowl.

3. Dissolve cornstarch in 1 tablespoon water.

To Cook:

1. Heat 2 tablespoons oil in a wok over high heat. Add garlic, ginger root, then pork; stir-fry for 2 minutes.

2. Carefully add bean curd and the seasoning sauce, stirring very gently. Bring to a boil and cook for another minute.

3. Add cornstarch mixture and sesame oil. When thickened, transfer to a serving dish; sprinkle with chopped green onion.

Stuffed Bean Curd (Serves 2 to 3)   釀 豆 腐

> 2 ounces small shrimp in shells
> 4 ounces lean ground pork

> *Marinade for shrimp and pork:*
>> Dash white pepper
>> 1 tablespoon chopped green onion
>> ¼ teaspoon salt
>> 2 teaspoons cornstarch
>> 1 teaspoon dry sherry
>> 2 teaspoons soy sauce
>> 2 tablespoons water

> 4 squares firm bean curd

> *Sauce:*
>> 1 tablespoon soy sauce
>> 2 tablespoons oyster sauce
>> 1 cup chicken broth

> 1 teaspoon cornstarch
> 3 tablespoons oil

Garnish: sprigs of cilantro or shredded green onions

To Prepare Ahead:

1. Shell, devein, and rinse shrimp. Chop shrimp until pasty and transfer to a small mixing bowl.

2. Add pork and marinade ingredients to the shrimp; stir in a circular motion for 2 to 3 minutes.

3. Cut each bean curd square into 4 triangles. Cut a slit on the long side of the triangle and carefully remove 2 teaspoons of bean curd.

4. Stuff 1 tablespoon of the ground pork mixture into each slit.

5. Combine sauce ingredients in a bowl.

6. Mix 1 teaspoon cornstarch and 1 tablespoon water in a small bowl; set aside.

To Cook:

1. Heat 3 tablespoons oil in a large, non-stick skillet. Lay stuffed bean curd triangles, meat-side down, and brown for 3 minutes over medium heat.

2. Add sauce mixture, cover, and cook for 5 minutes. After cooking, there should be about ⅓ cup liquid left. (If too much liquid remains, turn heat to high and cook uncovered until the excess liquid boils off.) Remove skillet from the heat.

3. Using a spatula carefully transfer the bean curd triangles to a plate, leaving the liquid in the skillet.

4. Add cornstarch mixture to skillet; stir until thickened. Pour the sauce over the bean curd. Garnish with cilantro or green onions.

Egg Foo Yung with Barbecued Pork (Yields 7 "pancakes," serves 2)

4 eggs
1 cup fresh mung bean sprouts
1 cup diced fresh mushrooms
½ cup diced barbecued pork (page 98)

叉燒蓉蛋

Sauce:
Dash freshly ground pepper
1 tablespoon cornstarch
½ cup chicken broth
¼ cup water
2 teaspoons soy sauce

5 tablespoons oil
½ teaspoon salt
1 green onion, chopped

To Prepare Ahead:

1. Beat eggs lightly and set aside.

2. Rinse and drain bean sprouts. Pile on a chopping board and cut into 1-inch lengths.

3. Combine sauce ingredients in a small saucepan.

To Cook:

1. Heat 1 tablespoon oil in a wok over high heat. Add bean sprouts, mushrooms, salt, and pork; stir-fry for 1 minute. Add to the eggs.

2. Rinse and dry the wok. Add 1 tablespoon oil; when hot, add ¼ cup egg mixture. Reduce heat to medium, cook undisturbed for 30 seconds or until brown on bottom. Flip over and cook for another 30 seconds. Transfer to a warm plate.

3. Add ½ tablespoon oil and ¼ cup egg mixture for each additional pancake, and repeat the cooking procedure.

4. Bring the sauce mixture to a boil over high heat, stirring constantly. Sprinkle with chopped green onion and pour over the pancakes.

Egg Foo Yung with Shrimp (Yields 7 "Pancakes," serves 2)

4 eggs
¼ pound small shrimp in shells
½ cup green peas, fresh or frozen
1 cup diced fresh mushrooms
1 cup fresh mung bean sprouts

蝦仁蓉蛋

Sauce:
    Dash freshly ground pepper
    1 tablespoon cornstarch
    ¼ cup water
    ½ cup chicken broth
    2 tablespoons oyster sauce

6 tablespoons oil
1 green onion, chopped
½ teaspoon salt

To Prepare Ahead:

1. Beat eggs lightly and set aside.

2. Shell and devein shrimp. Cut into pieces the size of peas.

3. Cook peas in 1 cup of boiling water for 1 to 2 minutes; drain and set aside.

4. Rinse and drain bean sprouts. Pile on a chopping board and cut into 1-inch lengths.

5. Combine sauce ingredients in a small saucepan.

To Cook:

1. Heat 2 tablespoons oil in a wok over high heat. Add chopped green onion and shrimp; stir-fry for 1 minute. Scatter in bean sprouts, mushrooms, and ½ teaspoon salt; stir-fry for another minute. Add to the eggs.

2. Rinse and dry the wok. Add 1 tablespoon oil; when hot, add ¼ cup egg mixture. Reduce heat to medium; cook undisturbed for 30 seconds or until brown on bottom. Flip over and cook for another 30 seconds. Transfer to a warm plate.

3. Add ½ tablespoon oil and ¼ cup egg mixture for each additional pancake, and repeat the cooking procedure.

4. Bring the sauce mixture to a boil over high heat, stirring constantly. Add peas and pour over the pancakes.

Agar-Agar Salad (Serves 4)　涼拌洋菜

　　½ ounce dried agar-agar
　　1 cucumber
　　½ cup shredded cooked chicken
　　1 cup shredded carrot
　　½ cup shredded cooked Virginia ham
　　　or other cooked ham

Salad dressing:
　　1 tablespoon mustard powder
　　½ teaspoon salt
　　1 tablespoon sugar
　　2 tablespoons vinegar
　　2 tablespoons soy sauce
　　2 tablespoons peanut butter
　　1 tablespoon sesame oil

1. With a pair of scissors, cut agar-agar into 2-inch pieces. Soak in tap water for 10 minutes; rinse and squeeze dry.

2. Peel, seed, and shred the cucumber.

3. Combine agar-agar, cucumber, chicken, and carrot in a dish. Spread ham on top; cover and refrigerate for 1 hour.

4. To make the salad dressing: In a small bowl, mix mustard powder with 2 tablespoons water until creamy. Add the remaining ingredients and mix thoroughly.

5. Just before serving, pour salad dressing over the salad.

Tip ● This salad will keep in the refrigerator for a couple of days.

Stir-Fried Vegetables (Serves 2)　炒 素 菜

　　1 onion
　　4 ounces fresh mushrooms
　　4 ounces fresh snow peas

Thickening sauce:
　　1 teaspoon cornstarch
　　½ teaspoon sugar
　　2 tablespoons chicken broth
　　1 tablespoon oyster sauce
　　¼ teaspoon sesame oil

　　3 tablespoons oil
　　¾ teaspoon salt

To Prepare Ahead:

1. Cut onion into 8 wedges and separate into layers.

2. Rinse, drain, and cut mushrooms into ½-inch slices.

3. Rinse, and remove tips and strings from snow peas.

4. Combine ingredients for thickening sauce in a small bowl.

To Cook:

1. Heat 3 tablespoons oil in a wok over high heat. Add onion, mushrooms, snow peas, and salt; stir-fry for 2 to 3 minutes.

2. Add thickening sauce; stir until thickened and serve.

Stir-Fried Bean Sprouts (Serves 2)　炒 銀 芽

　　1 pound fresh mung bean sprouts

　　Thickening sauce:
　　　　1 teaspoon cornstarch
　　　　½ teaspoon sugar
　　　　1 teaspoon soy sauce
　　　　1 teaspoon sesame oil
　　　　3 tablespoons chicken broth

　　4 tablespoons oil
　　1 clove garlic, smashed and peeled
　　2 green onions, shredded
　　1 teaspoon salt

To Prepare Ahead:

1. Rinse bean sprouts in a large pot of cold water and drain.

2. Combine ingredients for thickening sauce in a small bowl.

To Cook:

1. Heat 4 tablespoons oil in a wok over high heat. Add garlic, then green onions, bean sprouts, and salt. Stir-fry for 2 minutes.

2. Remove garlic and excess liquid; add thickening sauce. Stir until thickened and serve.

Cucumber Salad (Serves 4)　涼拌黄瓜

    1 pound cucumbers (about 2)
    1 teaspoon salt

Salad dressing:
    1 tablespoon sugar
    1 tablespoon sesame seed paste
     or peanut butter
    1 teaspoon soy sauce
    1 tablespoon sesame oil
    2 tablespoons white vinegar

1. Peel cucumbers and cut in half lengthwise; remove seeds. Cut diagonally into ⅛-inch-thick slices. Place in a mixing bowl. Sprinkle with salt and mix well; refrigerate for an hour.

2. Combine salad dressing ingredients in a small bowl; blend well.

3. Drain liquid from cucumber and add salad dressing. Mix thoroughly; cover and refrigerate for 30 minutes before serving.

4. To serve, drain off most of the liquid and transfer to a serving dish.

Tips • This salad can be served as part of a cold plate.

       • For a different taste, omit the peanut butter or sesame seed paste.

Stir-Fried Chinese Cabbage (Serves 2)　炒白菜

    1½ pounds Chinese cabbage
    3 tablespoons oil
    1 teaspoon salt

1. Rinse Chinese cabbage and drain thoroughly. Cut crosswise into 1-inch pieces.

2. Heat 3 tablespoons oil in a wok over high heat; add cabbage and salt; stir-fry for 4 to 5 minutes.

Tip • For a richer flavor, add 2 tablespoons cooked chicken fat to the cabbage at the end of cooking and mix thoroughly.

Sweet and Sour Radishes (Serves 8)　糖醋小紅蘿蔔

> 2 (6-ounce) packages radishes
> ½ teaspoon salt
> 3 tablespoons sugar
> 3 tablespoons white vinegar
> 1 tablespoon sesame oil

1. Cut off ends of radishes; wash.

2. Lay each radish on its side. With a cleaver or small sharp knife, make parallel cuts ⅛ inch apart and about ⅔ of the way through the radish.

3. In a mixing bowl, combine radishes with salt. Refrigerate for an hour. Pour off liquid.

4. Add sugar, vinegar, and sesame oil; mix well. Store in the refrigerator for an hour and serve. (See picture on pages 18 and 19.)

Tip • You can store the marinated radishes in the refrigerator overnight. However, although storing improves the flavor, the red color of the radish skin will dissolve in the liquid, and they will not look as attractive.

Tangy Cabbage (Serves 6)　麻辣包心菜

> 1 pound cabbage
> 1 teaspoon salt
> ¼ cup sugar
> ¼ cup white vinegar
> 2 tablespoons oil
> 2 tablespoons sesame oil
> 4 slices peeled ginger root
> 1 teaspoon Szechwan peppercorns
> 1 teaspoon dried chili pepper flakes

1. Wash, drain, and shred the cabbage. Sprinkle with salt and mix well. Refrigerate for 2 hours; discard the liquid.

2. Dissolve sugar in vinegar. Add to the cabbage; mix well.

3. Heat oil and sesame oil in a small saucepan over high heat. Add ginger root, Szechwan peppercorns, and dried chili pepper flakes. Cook until the ginger root turns brown.

4. Pour through a sieve over the cabbage mixture; toss together thoroughly.

5. Cover and refrigerate for 3 hours before serving.

Tip • Tangy cabbage will keep in the refrigerator for 3 to 4 days.

Table for Stir-Frying Fresh Vegetables

General Cooking Instructions:

1. Cut vegetable as directed.
2. Heat oil; add seasoning, vegetable, and salt; cook for the designated time. If chicken broth is required, add it in the middle of cooking unless otherwise instructed. (See * items.)
3. If thickening sauce is required, add after cooking time. When it thickens, serve the vegetable immediately.

Vegetable	Amount	Cutting Technique	Temperature	Oil	Seasoning	Salt	Chicken broth	Cooking Time (minutes)	Thickening Sauce
Asparagus	1 lb	roll-cut	high	2 T	-	¾ t	-	2	-
Bean sprouts (mung)	1 lb	-	high	4 T	2 cloves garlic	1 t	-	1-2	1 t cornstarch 2 T chicken broth
Bell pepper	3	slice	high	2 T		½ t	1 T	2	-
Bok choy	1½ lbs	slice	high	3 T		1 t	-	3	1 t cornstarch 3 T chicken broth
Broccoli	1 lb	slice (stems) bite-sized flowerets	high	3 T	-	1 t	1 T	3	1 t cornstarch 2 T chicken broth
Cabbage	1 lb	shred	high-med.*	3 T	-	1 t	¼ C*	5	-

78

Vegetable	Amount	Cut	Heat	Oil	Garlic				Sauce
Carrot	1 lb	shred or slice	high	2 T	-	½ t	2 T	3	1 t cornstarch 2 T chicken broth
Cauliflower	1 lb	bite-sized flowerets	high-med.*	3 T	-	1 t	¼ C*	3	1 t cornstarch 2 T milk
Celery	1 lb	slice	high	2 T	-	½ t	-	2	-
Chinese cabbage	1½ lbs	1" pieces	high	3 T	-	1 t	-	5	1 t cornstarch 1 T chicken broth
Cucumber	1 lb	slice	high	2 T	-	½ t	-	2	-
Eggplant	1½ lbs	1" chunks	high-med.*	3 T	2 cloves garlic	1 t	½ C*	8-10	1 t cornstarch 1 T soy sauce 2 T chicken broth
Green beans	1 lb	cut diagonally	high-med.*	3 T	-	1 t	¼ C*	6	-
Iceberg lettuce	1 lb	shred	high	3 T	1 clove garlic	½ t	-	1-2	-
Mushrooms	1 lb	slice (½" thick)	high	4 T	-	1 t	-	2	1 t cornstarch 1 T chicken broth 1 T oyster sauce
Romaine lettuce	1 lb	1" pieces	high	3 T	1 clove garlic	½ t	-	2	1 t cornstarch 1 T chicken broth
Snow peas	¾ lb	-	high	2 T	-	½ t	1 T	2	-
Spinach	1 lb	1" pieces	high	3 T	1 clove garlic	½ t	-	2	1 t cornstarch ½ t sugar 1 T chicken broth
Zucchini	1 lb	slice	high	3 T	-	¾ t	1 T	2-3	1 t cornstarch 2 t soy sauce 2 T chicken broth

* Stir-fry 1 minute over high heat, reduce heat to medium, and add chicken broth. Cover and finish cooking over medium heat.

Szechwan Eggplant (Serves 2)   魚香茄子

1½ pounds eggplant

Seasoning sauce:
    1 tablespoon sugar
    2 teaspoons cornstarch
    2 tablespoons chicken broth
    2 tablespoons hot bean sauce
    1 tablespoon soy sauce
    1 tablespoon dry sherry
    1 tablespoon cider vinegar
    1 teaspoon sesame oil

3 tablespoons oil
¼ teaspoon minced ginger root
2 teaspoons minced garlic
¼ pound lean ground pork
½ teaspoon salt
½ cup chicken broth
2 green onions, chopped

To Prepare Ahead:

1. Rinse the eggplant. If they are small, the peel will be tender and you do not have to peel them; if they are large with tough skin, peel them first.

2. Cut eggplant into 1-inch chunks.

3. Mix ingredients for seasoning sauce in a small bowl.

To Cook:

1. Heat 3 tablespoons oil in a wok over high heat. Add ginger root, garlic, and ground pork; stir for 1 minute.

2. Add eggplant and salt, stirring constantly for 1 minute. Add chicken broth, turn heat to medium, cover, and cook for 8 to 10 minutes.

3. Add sauce mixture and chopped green onions; stir until thickened and serve.

Tip   •   This dish can be cooked ahead; it tastes delicious when reheated.

Beef

Beef with Barbecue Sauce (Serves 3 to 4)　沙茶牛肉

1 pound flank steak

Marinade for beef:
- 1 tablespoon cornstarch
- 1 tablespoon water
- 1 tablespoon oil
- 2 tablespoons soy sauce
- 2 teaspoons dry sherry

1 teaspoon cornstarch
3 tablespoons oil
1 clove garlic, smashed and peeled
¼ teaspoon salt
1½ tablespoons barbecue sauce

To Prepare Ahead:

1. Cut flank steak lengthwise into strips 1½ inches wide; then cut across the grain into ⅛-inch slices.

2. Transfer beef slices to a mixing bowl. Add marinade ingredients and toss to coat thoroughly; let stand for 30 minutes or longer.

3. Mix 1 teaspoon cornstarch with ¼ cup water.

To Cook:

1. Heat 3 tablespoons oil in a wok over high heat. Add garlic; after a few seconds, add beef slices and stir-fry for 1 minute.

2. Add salt and barbecue sauce. Stir-fry for 1 more minute. Discard the garlic.

3. Pour in cornstarch mixture; stir for a few seconds and serve.

Beef and Mushrooms in Hot Bean Sauce (Serves 2) 辣醬牛肉

½ pound flank steak

Marinade for beef:
    2 teaspoons cornstarch
    2 teaspoons water
    1 teaspoon dry sherry
    1 tablespoon oil
    1 tablespoon soy sauce

½ pound fresh mushrooms

Seasoning sauce:
    1 teaspoon cornstarch
    3 tablespoons water
    1 to 2 tablespoons hot bean sauce

4 tablespoons oil
½ teaspoon salt
3 green onions, cut into 1½-inch pieces

To Prepare Ahead:

1. Cut flank steak lengthwise into strips 1½ inches wide; then cut across the grain into ⅛-inch slices.

2. Transfer beef slices to a mixing bowl. Add marinade ingredients and toss to coat thoroughly. Let stand for 30 minutes or longer.

3. Rinse and slice mushrooms ½ inch thick.

4. Mix the ingredients for seasoning sauce in a small bowl.

To Cook:

1. Heat 2 tablespoons oil in a wok over high heat. Add mushrooms and salt, and stir-fry for 1 minute. Transfer to a plate.

2. Add 2 tablespoons oil to the wok. When hot, add green onions and beef mixture. Stir-fry for 1 to 2 minutes.

3. Return mushrooms to the wok and pour in sauce. Stir a few seconds and serve.

Braised Star Anise Beef and Eggs (Serves 6 to 10)　　滷牛肉與蛋

            3 whole star anise
              or an equal amount of broken pieces
            10 Szechwan peppercorns
            ½ cinnamon stick
            3 cloves garlic, smashed and peeled
            2 slices peeled ginger root
            2 green onions, cut into 2-inch pieces
            1 teaspoon salt
            1 tablespoon sugar
            2 tablespoons dry sherry
            ½ cup soy sauce
            2 cups water

            3 to 4 pounds whole, boned beef shank
            6 hard boiled eggs, shelled
            1 teaspoon sesame oil

Garnish: radish fans (page 176) and sprigs of cilantro

The Day Before:

1. Put all ingredients except beef, eggs, and sesame oil in a heavy 4- to 6-quart saucepan and bring to a boil over high heat.

2. Add beef shank, reduce heat to medium-low, cover and cook for about 2 hours. Turn beef over a couple of times during cooking. There should be about 1 cup of cooking liquid left.

3. Transfer beef to a serving dish, leaving sauce in the saucepan.

4. Add shelled eggs to the saucepan and cook for 15 minutes over medium heat, basting several times with the sauce during cooking. Remove the eggs.

5. Strain the sauce, cool to room temperature, and store in a covered container.

6. Refrigerate beef, eggs, and sauce separately overnight.

To Serve:

1. Before serving, cut beef crosswise into paper-thin slices and arrange attractively in overlapping layers on a platter. (See picture on pages 18 and 19.)

2. Halve or quarter eggs and arrange them with the beef on the platter.

3. Remove fat from sauce. Warm ¼ cup of sauce in a small saucepan, add 1 teaspoon sesame oil and pour over the beef slices. Garnish and serve.

Tip • Freeze the rest of sauce for later use. Leftover beef slices are great for sandwiches.

Dry-Sautéed Beef Shreds (Serves 3 to 4) 乾煸牛肉絲

1 pound flank steak

Marinade for beef:
    1 teaspoon sugar
    ½ teaspoon minced ginger root
    1 tablespoon hot bean sauce
    1 tablespoon dry sherry
    2 tablespoons soy sauce

2 small fresh hot peppers
4 tablespoons oil
1 cup shredded carrot
1 cup shredded celery
¼ teaspoon salt
Dash freshly ground pepper
1 teaspoon sesame oil

To Prepare Ahead:

1. Cut flank steak crosswise into strips 1½ inches wide; then slice and shred it with the grain into strips about ¼ x ¼ x 1½ inches.

2. Transfer beef shreds to a mixing bowl. Add marinade ingredients and toss to coat thoroughly. Let stand for 30 minutes or longer.

3. Cut peppers in half lengthwise; remove seeds and shred into thin strips.

To Cook:

1. Heat 1 tablespoon oil in a wok over high heat. Add carrot shreds; stir-fry for 1 minute. Add celery and salt; stir for another minute. Transfer to a plate.

2. Wipe the wok with a paper towel; heat 3 tablespoons oil, add peppers and beef mixture. Stir-fry over high heat for 6 minutes.

3. Reduce heat to medium and cook for another 6 minutes, or until all the liquid has evaporated, stirring occasionally.

4. Return vegetables to the wok. Sprinkle with pepper and sesame oil. Mix well and serve.

Tip • You can cook this dish a day in advance and refrigerate. Serve at room temperature or reheat in a microwave oven.

Foil-Wrapped Beef Slices (Serves 2)   錫紙包牛肉

½ pound flank steak

Marinade for beef:
   1 tablespoon cornstarch
   1 tablespoon soy sauce
   1 tablespoon dry sherry
   1 tablespoon oyster sauce
   2 tablespoons oil
   Dash freshly ground pepper

1 onion
¼ teaspoon salt
2 green onions, chopped
1 tablespoon sesame oil
15 pieces aluminum foil, each 6 x 6 inches

To Prepare Ahead:

1. Cut flank steak lengthwise into 2 strips. Holding the cleaver at a 45° angle to the cutting board, slice flank steak across the grain into pieces about 1 x 2 inches and ¼ inch thick.

2. Transfer beef slices to a mixing bowl. Add marinade ingredients and toss to coat thoroughly.

3. Cut onion into ¼-inch-thick rings and sprinkle with salt.

4. Add onion rings and chopped green onions to beef mixture. Mix and let stand for 30 minutes.

To Wrap:

1. Squirt 2 or 3 drops of sesame oil in the center of each aluminum foil square. Spread the oil to form a 1-inch circle, using chopsticks or a spoon.

2. Divide beef and onion rings among the pieces of foil. Fold as shown on page 121.

To Cook:

Preheat oven to 450°F. Place envelopes of beef on a cookie sheet and bake for 10 minutes.

To Serve:

Unwrap with fingers. Serve with rice.

Ginger Beef (Serves 2 to 3) 生薑牛肉

¾ pound flank steak

Marinade for beef:
  1 tablespoon cornstarch
  1 tablespoon oil
  2 tablespoons soy sauce
  2 teaspoons dry sherry
  1 tablespoon water

Thickening sauce:
  1 teaspoon cornstarch
  4 tablespoons water
  2 tablespoons oyster sauce
  ½ teaspoon sesame oil
  Dash freshly ground pepper

3 tablespoons oil
15 slices fresh, tender, peeled ginger root

To Prepare Ahead:

1. Cut flank steak lengthwise into strips 1½ inches wide; then cut across the grain into ⅛-inch slices.

2. Transfer beef slices to a mixing bowl. Add marinade ingredients and toss to coat thoroughly; let stand for 30 minutes or longer.

3. Mix ingredients for thickening sauce in a small bowl.

To Cook:

1. Heat 3 tablespoons oil in a wok over high heat. Add ginger root and beef slices. Stir-fry for about 2 minutes.

2. Add sauce mixture; stir until thickened and serve.

Ground Beef with Cellophane Noodles (Serves 2)　螞蟻上樹

2 ounces cellophane noodles

Seasoning sauce:
Dash freshly ground pepper
¼ teaspoon salt
1 teaspoon sugar
1 tablespoon cornstarch
1 tablespoon soy sauce
1 tablespoon hot bean sauce
1 teaspoon dry sherry
½ cup chicken broth
½ cup water
½ teaspoon sesame oil

3 cups oil for deep-frying
1 small fresh hot pepper, seeded and chopped
½ teaspoon minced ginger root
1 green onion, chopped
½ pound lean ground beef

To Prepare Ahead:

1. Separate cellophane noodles into 2 portions either by pulling apart or cutting with a pair of scissors.

2. Mix ingredients for seasoning sauce in a bowl.

To Cook:

1. Heat 3 cups oil in a wok over high heat. (To test the oil, dip a piece of cellophane noodle into the hot oil. If it puffs out immediately, the oil is hot enough.) Add half the dried cellophane noodles. When they puff up (in just a few seconds), drain and transfer noodles to a large bowl lined with paper towels.

2. Cook the other half of noodles the same way.

3. Remove all but 1 tablespoon oil from the wok. Add fresh hot pepper, ginger root, and green onion; stir a few seconds. Add beef and stir-fry until done.

4. Add seasoning sauce, stirring constantly until it comes to a boil.

5. Remove paper towels from the cellophane noodles and pour sauce over them. Mix well and transfer to a plate. Serve with rice.

Pepper Steak I (Serves 2)　青椒牛肉

　　½ pound flank steak

　　Marinade for beef:
　　　2 teaspoons cornstarch
　　　2 teaspoons water
　　　1 teaspoon dry sherry
　　　1 tablespoon oil
　　　1 tablespoon soy sauce

　　2 bell peppers

　　Thickening sauce:
　　　½ teaspoon sugar
　　　1 teaspoon cornstarch
　　　2 tablespoons oyster sauce
　　　4 tablespoons water

　　3 tablespoons oil
　　¼ teaspoon salt *or* to taste
　　2 thin slices peeled ginger root

To Prepare Ahead:

1. Cut flank steak lengthwise into strips 1½ inches wide; then cut across the grain into ⅛-inch slices.

2. Transfer beef slices to a mixing bowl. Add marinade ingredients and toss to coat thoroughly. Let stand for 30 minutes or longer.

3. Seed peppers and cut into 1-inch squares.

4. Mix ingredients for thickening sauce in a small bowl.

To Cook:

1. Add 1 tablespoon oil to a wok over high heat. Swirl the oil and heat for 30 seconds. Add pepper squares and salt, and stir-fry for 1 minute or until tender but still crisp. (Add 1 tablespoon water if it gets too dry.) Transfer to a plate.

2. Wipe the wok with a paper towel; pour in 2 tablespoons oil. When hot, add ginger root; after a few seconds, add steak mixture. Stir-fry over high heat for 1 to 2 minutes. Discard the ginger root.

3. Return pepper squares to the wok and pour in sauce. Stir until thickened and serve.

Pepper Steak II (Serves 2)　青椒蕃茄牛肉

½ pound flank steak

Marinade for beef:
    2 teaspoons cornstarch
    2 teaspoons water
    1 teaspoon dry sherry
    1 tablespoon oil
    1 tablespoon soy sauce

1 bell pepper
1 tomato
1 onion

Thickening sauce:
    1 teaspoon cornstarch
    ½ teaspoon sugar
    3 tablespoons water
    2 tablespoons oyster sauce

4 tablespoons oil
½ teaspoon salt
1 clove garlic, smashed and peeled

To Prepare Ahead:

1. Cut flank steak lengthwise into strips 1½ inches wide; then cut across the grain into ⅛-inch slices.

2. Transfer beef slices to a mixing bowl. Add marinade ingredients and toss to coat thoroughly. Let stand for 30 minutes or longer.

3. Seed bell pepper and cut into ½ x 2-inch pieces. Cut tomato and onion into 8 wedges; separate onion into layers.

4. Mix ingredients for thickening sauce in a small bowl.

To Cook:

1. Add 1 tablespoon oil to a wok over high heat and swirl. When hot, add onion and stir-fry for 1 minute.

2. Add bell pepper and salt, stir-fry for 1 minute and remove to a plate.

3. Wipe the wok with a paper towel; pour in 3 tablespoons oil. When hot, add garlic; after a few seconds, add steak mixture. When steak is half-cooked, add tomato. Cook 1 more minute. Discard the garlic.

4. Return pepper and onion to the wok, and pour in sauce. Stir until thickened and serve.

Scallion Beef (Serves 2 to 3)   葱爆牛肉

¾ pound flank steak

Marinade for beef:
1 tablespoon cornstarch
1 tablespoon water
1 tablespoon oil
2 tablespoons soy sauce
2 teaspoons dry sherry

1 bunch green onions

Thickening sauce:
1 teaspoon cornstarch
4 tablespoons water
2 tablespoons oyster sauce
¼ teaspoon sesame oil

3 tablespoons oil
2 slices peeled ginger root
¼ teaspoon salt

To Prepare Ahead:

1. Cut flank steak lengthwise into strips 1½ inches wide; then cut across the grain into ⅛-inch slices.

2. Transfer beef slices to a mixing bowl. Add marinade ingredients and toss to coat thoroughly; let stand for 30 minutes or longer.

3. Rinse and cut green onions into 2-inch pieces.

4. Mix ingredients for thickening sauce in a small bowl.

To Cook:

1. Heat 3 tablespoons oil in a wok over high heat. Add ginger root; after a few seconds, add beef slices, green onions and salt. Stir-fry for 2 minutes. Discard the ginger root.

2. Pour in sauce; stir until thickened and serve.

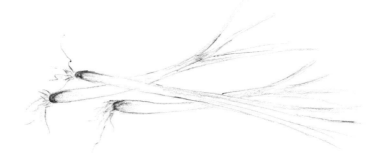

Shredded Beef with Onion (Serves 2)　　洋葱牛肉絲

½ pound flank steak

Marinade for beef:
    2 teaspoons cornstarch
    2 teaspoons water
    1 teaspoon dry sherry
    1 tablespoon oil
    1 tablespoon soy sauce

2 onions

Thickening sauce:
    2 teaspoons cornstarch
    ½ teaspoon sugar
    2 teaspoons soy sauce
    5 tablespoons water

3 tablespoons oil
½ teaspoon salt

To Prepare Ahead:

1. Cut flank steak lengthwise into strips 1½ inches wide; then cut across the grain into ⅛-inch slices; shred the slices into strips about ⅛ x ⅛ x 1½ inches.

2. Transfer beef shreds to a mixing bowl. Add marinade ingredients and toss to coat thoroughly; let stand for 30 minutes or longer.

3. Cut onions in half and shred lengthwise.

4. Mix ingredients for thickening sauce in a small bowl.

To Cook:

1. Place the wok over high heat, pour in 1 tablespoon oil, and swirl. When hot, add onions and salt. Stir-fry for 2 to 3 minutes; transfer to a plate.

2. Wipe the wok with a paper towel and pour in 2 tablespoons oil. When hot, add beef shreds. Stir-fry for 1 to 2 minutes.

3. Return onions to the wok and add sauce. Stir until thickened and serve.

Sliced Beef and Romaine Lettuce (Serves 2)　牛肉生菜

½ pound flank steak

Marinade for beef:
  2 teaspoons cornstarch
  2 teaspoons water
  1 teaspoon dry sherry
  1 tablespoon oil
  1 tablespoon soy sauce

1 small head Romaine lettuce

Thickening sauce:
  1 teaspoon cornstarch
  4 tablespoons water
  2 tablespoons oyster sauce

4 tablespoons oil
½ teaspoon salt
1 clove garlic, smashed and peeled

To Prepare Ahead:

1. Cut flank steak lengthwise into strips 1½ inches wide; then cut across the grain into ⅛-inch slices.

2. Transfer beef slices to a mixing bowl. Add marinade ingredients and toss to coat thoroughly. Let stand for 30 minutes or longer.

3. Wash and drain lettuce; cut crosswise into 1-inch pieces.

4. Mix ingredients for thickening sauce in a small bowl.

To Cook:

1. Heat 2 tablespoons oil in a wok over high heat. Add lettuce and salt; stir-fry for 1 to 2 minutes. Discard all liquid and transfer lettuce to a plate.

2. Wipe the wok with a paper towel and pour in 2 tablespoons oil. When hot, add garlic; a few seconds later, add beef mixture. Stir-fry for 1 to 2 minutes. Discard the garlic.

3. Add sauce to the wok and stir a few seconds. Pour over lettuce and serve.

Stir-Fried Beef with Asparagus (Serves 2) 蘆筍牛肉

½ pound flank steak

Marinade for beef:
    2 teaspoons cornstarch
    2 teaspoons water
    1 teaspoon dry sherry
    1 tablespoon oil
    1 tablespoon soy sauce

1 pound fresh asparagus

Thickening sauce:
    1 teaspoon cornstarch
    2 teaspoons soy sauce
    4 tablespoons water

4 tablespoons oil
¾ teaspoon salt *or* to taste
1 clove garlic, smashed and peeled

To Prepare Ahead:

1. Cut flank steak lengthwise into strips 1½ inches wide; then cut across the grain into ⅛-inch slices.

2. Transfer beef slices to a mixing bowl. Add marinade ingredients and toss to coat thoroughly; let stand for 30 minutes or longer.

3. Snap off tough ends of the asparagus. Rinse in a pot of cold water. Roll-cut into 1½-inch pieces.

4. Mix ingredients for thickening sauce in a small bowl.

To Cook:

1. Heat 2 tablespoons oil in a wok over high heat. Add asparagus and salt, and stir-fry for about 2 minutes. Transfer to a plate.

2. Wipe the wok with a paper towel and pour in 2 tablespoons oil. When hot, add garlic; after a few seconds, add beef mixture and stir-fry for 1 to 2 minutes. Discard the garlic.

3. Return asparagus to the wok and pour in sauce. Stir until thickened and serve.

Stir-Fried Beef with Broccoli (Serves 2)　　玉蘭牛肉

½ pound flank steak

Marinade for beef:
    2 teaspoons cornstarch
    1 teaspoon dry sherry
    2 teaspoons water
    1 tablespoon oil
    1 tablespoon soy sauce

1 pound fresh broccoli

Thickening sauce:
    1 teaspoon cornstarch
    ½ teaspoon sugar
    4 tablespoons water
    2 tablespoons oyster sauce

4 tablespoons oil
½ teaspoon salt
2 slices peeled ginger root

To Prepare Ahead:

1. Cut flank steak lengthwise into strips 1½ inches wide; then cut across the grain into ⅛-inch slices.

2. Transfer beef slices to a mixing bowl. Add marinade ingredients and toss to coat thoroughly. Let stand for 30 minutes or longer.

3. Wash and drain broccoli. Peel tough skin from the bottom of the stems with a paring knife. Cut each stalk into 3 or 4 equal sections. Slice stem sections lengthwise into ¼-inch pieces. Separate the flowerets into bite-sized pieces.

4. Mix ingredients for thickening sauce in a small bowl.

To Cook:

1. Heat 2 tablespoons oil in a wok over high heat. Add broccoli and salt, and stir-fry for 3 minutes. (Add 1 tablespoon water if it gets too dry.) Transfer to a plate.

2. Wipe the wok with a paper towel and add 2 tablespoons oil. When hot, add ginger root; after a few seconds, add beef mixture. Stir-fry over high heat for 1 to 2 minutes. Discard the ginger root.

3. Return broccoli to the wok and pour in sauce. Stir until thickened and serve. (See picture on pages 22 and 23.)

Stir-Fried Beef with Snow Peas (Serves 2)　雪豆牛肉

½ pound flank steak

Marinade for beef:
　2 teaspoons cornstarch
　2 teaspoons water
　1 teaspoon dry sherry
　1 tablespoon oil
　1 tablespoon soy sauce

½ pound fresh snow peas

Thickening sauce:
　1 teaspoon cornstarch
　3 tablespoons water
　1 tablespoon oyster sauce
　　or 2 teaspoons soy sauce

4 tablespoons oil
½ teaspoon salt
2 slices peeled ginger root

To Prepare Ahead:

1. Cut flank steak lengthwise into strips 1½ inches wide; then cut across the grain into ⅛-inch slices.

2. Transfer beef slices to a mixing bowl. Add marinade ingredients and toss to coat thoroughly. Let stand for 30 minutes or longer.

3. Wash snow peas and remove the tips and strings.

4. Mix ingredients for thickening sauce in a small bowl.

To Cook:

1. Heat 2 tablespoons oil in a wok over high heat. Add snow peas and salt, and stir-fry for 2 minutes. (If it gets too dry or starts to burn, add 1 tablespoon water.) Transfer to a plate.

2. Wipe the wok with a paper towel and pour in 2 tablespoons oil. When hot, add ginger root; after a few seconds, add beef mixture. Stir-fry for 1 to 2 minutes. Discard the ginger root.

3. Return snow peas to the wok and add sauce. Stir until thickened and serve.

Pork

Barbecued Pork (Serves 6)　叉　燒

　　　3 pounds pork*

　　　Marinade for pork:
　　　　1¼ teaspoons salt
　　　　1 teaspoon five-spice powder
　　　　3 tablespoons hoisin sauce
　　　　　or Chinese barbecue sauce
　　　　3 tablespoons soy sauce
　　　　2 tablespoons dry sherry
　　　　1 tablespoon honey
　　　　1 tablespoon oil
　　　　3 cloves garlic, finely minced

To Prepare Ahead:

1. Trim fat off pork and cut into pieces about the size of pork chops ¾ inch thick. (If using pork tenderloin, cut in half lengthwise.)

2. Combine the marinade ingredients in a large mixing bowl; mix thoroughly.

3. Dip each piece of pork into the marinade to coat well. Cover and refrigerate for 4 hours or overnight.

To Cook:

Place pork on a barbecue grill over medium heat and barbecue for about 30 minutes or until fully cooked, turning once or twice while cooking. During the last 10 minutes, baste with the marinade.

To Serve:

Slice barbecued pork pieces about ¾ x 2 inches and ⅛ inch thick. Serve hot or cold as part of a Chinese cold plate. (See picture on pages 18 and 19.)

Tips　• Barbecued pork has the best flavor when cooked over charcoal, but it can also be cooked in the oven. Line the roasting pan with foil and add some water to prevent smoking. Put the pan on the lower rack. Place the pork on the upper rack, 3 inches from the heat source. Broil pork pieces 2 minutes on each side. Brush with marinade; reduce heat to 350° F. and roast for 30 minutes.

　　　• Divide leftover pork into 4-ounce packages and freeze.

　　　• You can substitute barbecued pork for fresh meat in many stir-fried dishes, such as **Stir-Fried Barbecued Pork with Broccoli** (page 103).

---

* Use pork shoulder, boneless pork roast, or tenderloin.

Mu Hsu Pork (Serves 4)　木樨肉

½ pound lean pork*

Marinade for pork:
Dash freshly ground pepper
¼ teaspoon minced ginger root
2 teaspoons cornstarch
1 teaspoon dry sherry
1 tablespoon soy sauce

6 Chinese dried mushrooms
¼ cup dried black cloud ears
25 dried tiger lily buds
4 ounces fresh mung bean sprouts
2 eggs

Sauce:
1 teaspoon cornstarch
1 tablespoon soy sauce
4 tablespoons water
　or chicken broth
½ teaspoon sesame oil

6 tablespoons oil
½ teaspoon salt
2 green onions, shredded

To Prepare Ahead:

1. Shred pork by slicing it ⅛ inch thick across the grain; then cut the slices into strips about ⅛ x ⅛ x 2 inches.

2. Transfer pork shreds to a mixing bowl. Add marinade ingredients and toss to coat thoroughly; let stand for 30 minutes or longer.

3. Soak mushrooms and black cloud ears in 2 cups hot water for 20 minutes. Discard the water. Rinse and remove stems; shred the rest into thin strips.

4. Soak tiger lily buds in a cup of hot water for 10 minutes. Discard the water. Snap off hard ends of the buds. Rinse and cut each bud in half. Set aside with mushrooms and black cloud ears.

5. Rinse the bean sprouts in a pot of cold water and drain thoroughly.

6. Beat eggs lightly.

7. Mix sauce ingredients in a small bowl.

To Cook:

1. Place a 10- to 12-inch non-stick skillet over medium heat. Add 1 tablespoon

* Use pork tenderloin, butterfly pork chops, or boneless pork roast

oil, swirl. When hot, pour in the eggs, and tilt the skillet so that the whole surface is covered with a thin coat of egg. Flip the egg sheet over and cook for a few seconds. Transfer to a plate; when cool, shred into narrow strips 2 inches long.

2. Heat 2 tablespoons oil in a wok over high heat. Add bean sprouts, mushrooms, cloud ears, tiger lily buds, and salt. Stir-fry for 2 minutes and set aside with the eggs.

3. Wipe the wok with a paper towel and pour in 3 tablespoons oil. When hot, add green onions and pork; stir-fry for 3 minutes or until the pork is fully cooked.

4. Return the vegetables and eggs to the wok; add sauce and stir until thickened.

To Serve:

Serve with **Mandarin Pancakes** (page 168) or rice. To serve with the pancakes: peel the pair of pancakes apart. At the table, each guest fills his own pancake* with about 2 heaping tablespoons of Mu Hsu Pork and wraps it as shown below:

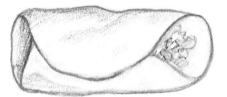

To eat from this end.

---

* A thin coat of hoisin sauce may be spread on the pancake before adding Mu Hsu Pork.

Shredded Pork with Bean Sprouts (Serves 2)　銀芽肉絲

½ pound lean pork*

Marinade for pork:
    2 teaspoons cornstarch
    1 teaspoon dry sherry
    1 tablespoon soy sauce
    Dash freshly ground pepper

½ pound fresh mung bean sprouts

Thickening sauce:
    1 teaspoon cornstarch
    2 teaspoons soy sauce
    2 tablespoons water
    ½ teaspoon sesame oil

5 tablespoons oil
½ teaspoon salt
1 slice peeled ginger root
1 clove garlic, sliced
1 green onion, shredded

To Prepare Ahead:

1. Shred pork by slicing it ⅛ inch thick across the grain; then cut the slices into strips about ⅛ x ⅛ x 2 inches.

2. Transfer pork shreds to a mixing bowl. Add marinade ingredients and toss to coat thoroughly. Let stand for 30 minutes or longer.

3. Rinse bean sprouts in a pot of cold water and drain thoroughly.

4. Mix ingredients for thickening sauce in a small bowl.

To Cook:

1. Heat 2 tablespoons oil in a wok over high heat. Add bean sprouts and salt, and stir-fry for 1 to 2 minutes. Transfer to a plate.

2. Wipe the wok with a paper towel. Heat 3 tablespoons oil over high heat. Add ginger root, garlic, and pork. Stir-fry for 3 to 5 minutes or until the pork is fully cooked. Discard the ginger root.

3. Add green onion and return bean sprouts to the wok. Pour in thickening sauce; stir a few seconds and serve.

* Use pork tenderloin, butterfly pork chops, or boneless pork roast.

Sweet and Sour Pork (Serves 3 to 4)　　咕　嚕　肉

　　1 pound pork tenderloin
　　1½ teaspoons salt
　　1 tablespoon soy sauce
　　1 bell pepper
　　1 (4-ounce) jar maraschino cherries
　　4 canned pineapple rings

Batter:
　　1 egg, lightly beaten
　　¼ cup cornstarch
　　¼ cup flour
　　¼ cup chicken broth

Sweet and sour sauce:
　　1 tablespoon cornstarch
　　2 tablespoons sugar
　　3 tablespoons white vinegar
　　2 tablespoons water
　　3 tablespoons catsup
　　2 teaspoons soy sauce
　　¼ teaspoon sesame oil
　　⅓ cup pineapple juice
　　⅓ cup chicken broth

　　3 cups oil for deep-frying
　　1 tablespoon oil

To Prepare Ahead:

1. Cut pork into 1-inch cubes.

2. Transfer pork to a mixing bowl. Add 1 teaspoon salt and 1 tablespoon soy sauce; mix well.

3. Seed and cut bell pepper into 1-inch squares. Drain cherries and pineapple, reserving the pineapple juice. Cut pineapple rings into 8 wedges.

4. Mix batter ingredients until well blended.

5. Mix sauce ingredients in a small saucepan.

To Cook:

1. Add pork cubes to the batter and mix well.

2. Heat 3 cups oil in a wok over high heat to 375°F. Or you can test the oil by adding a drop of batter to the hot oil. If it comes to the surface immediately, the oil is hot enough.

3. Add half the coated pork cubes, one by one, to the hot oil. Deep-fry for 5 minutes, or until golden brown and fully cooked.

4. With a strainer, transfer pork to a platter lined with paper towels.

5. Deep-fry the rest of the pork cubes.

6. Transfer the oil to a heat-proof bowl. Wipe the wok with a paper towel.

7. Bring sweet and sour sauce to a boil over high heat, stirring occasionally. Cover and remove from heat.

8. Heat 1 tablespoon oil in the wok over high heat. Add bell pepper and ½ teaspoon salt, and stir fry for 1 minute. Add pineapple, cherries, and sauce; bring to a boil.

9. Remove paper towels from pork. Pour the sauce mixture over it and serve.

Tip • You can prepare this dish through cooking step 6 a day in advance. Cover and refrigerate. To reheat, spread deep-fried pork cubes on a cookie sheet. Preheat oven to 350°F. and bake for 10 minutes. Proceed to steps 7, 8, and 9.

Stir-Fried Barbecued Pork with Broccoli (Serves 2)   玉 蘭 叉 燒

¼ pound barbecued pork (page 98)
1 pound fresh broccoli

Thickening sauce:
    1 teaspoon cornstarch
    ½ teaspoon sugar
    2 teaspoons dry sherry
    3 tablespoons water
    2 tablespoons oyster sauce

3 tablespoons oil
1 teaspoon salt

To Prepare Ahead:

1. Slice barbecued pork across the grain into ⅛-inch slices.

2. With a paring knife, remove the tough skin from broccoli stems; rinse and drain. Cut each stalk into 3 or 4 sections. Slice stem sections lengthwise into ¼-inch pieces. Separate the flowerets into bite-sized pieces.

3. Mix ingredients for thickening sauce in a small bowl.

To Cook:

1. Heat 3 tablespoons oil in a wok over high heat. Add broccoli and salt; stir-fry for 3 minutes. (Add 1 tablespoon water if it gets too dry.)

2. Add pork to the wok and stir for 1 minute.

3. Pour in sauce, stir until thickened, and serve.

Twice-Cooked Pork (Serves 3 to 4)　　回 鍋 肉

    1 pound pork shoulder roast (boneless)
    1 teaspoon salt
    1 tablespoon dry sherry
    2 green onions, cut into 2-inch pieces
    2 slices peeled ginger root
    1 bell pepper
    1 fresh hot pepper*
    1 leek** (about ½ pound)

Seasoning sauce:
    2 teaspoons sugar
    1 tablespoon hot bean sauce
    1 tablespoon sweet bean sauce
    2 tablespoons soy sauce

    4 tablespoons oil
    ½ teaspoon salt
    2 cloves garlic, sliced

To Prepare Ahead:

1. In a 3- to 4-quart saucepan, bring 1 quart of water to a boil. Add pork, 1 teaspoon salt, dry sherry, green onions, and ginger root. Cover and cook over medium high heat for 15 minutes.

2. Remove pork from the pan and cool under cold running water. Drain pork and slice thinly across the grain. (The inside of the pork might still be raw.)

3. Seed and cut bell pepper into 1-inch squares. Cut hot pepper into ¼-inch circles; remove seeds.

4. Cut off leek root and cut leek in half lengthwise. Wash thoroughly and cut diagonally into 1-inch pieces.

5. Mix ingredients for seasoning sauce in a small bowl.

To Cook:

1. Heat 2 tablespoons oil in a wok over high heat. Stir-fry bell pepper and leek with ½ teaspoon salt for 2 minutes. Transfer to a plate.

2. Wipe the wok with a paper towel. Heat 2 tablespoons oil. Add garlic, hot pepper, and pork slices. Stir-fry for 3 minutes or until pork is fully cooked.

3. Add sauce mixture, stirring to coat the pork slices.

4. Return vegetables to the wok; mix well and serve. (See picture on pages 24 and 25.)

 * Add more hot peppers if you like it spicier.
** If leek is not available, substitute 2 cups sliced cabbage.

Shredded Pork with Spicy Sauce (Serves 2 to 3)   魚香肉絲

½ pound lean pork*

Marinade for pork:
    2 teaspoons cornstarch
    2 teaspoons dry sherry
    1 tablespoon soy sauce

¼ cup dried black cloud ears
10 water chestnuts
2 fresh hot peppers

Seasoning sauce:
    ½ teaspoon salt
    ⅛ teaspoon freshly ground pepper
    1 teaspoon sugar
    1 teaspoon cornstarch
    1 tablespoon soy sauce
    1 tablespoon hot bean sauce
    3 tablespoons water
    1 teaspoon sesame oil

5 tablespoons oil
½ teaspoon minced ginger root
1 green onion, shredded
1 teaspoon chopped garlic

To Prepare Ahead:

1. Shred pork by slicing it ⅛ inch thick across the grain; then cut the slices into strips about ⅛ x ⅛ x 2 inches.

2. Transfer pork shreds to a mixing bowl. Add marinade ingredients and toss to coat thoroughly; let stand for 30 minutes or longer.

3. Soak black cloud ears in 2 cups hot water until softened, about 20 minutes. Rinse and discard the tiny stems. Shred finely.

4. Slice and shred water chestnuts. Cut hot peppers in half lengthwise; remove seeds and shred.

5. Mix ingredients for seasoning sauce in a small bowl.

To Cook:

1. Heat 2 tablespoons oil in a wok over high heat. Add water chestnuts and cloud ears; stir-fry for 2 minutes. Transfer to a plate.

2. Heat 3 tablespoons oil in the wok over high heat. Add ginger root, hot peppers, green onion, garlic, and pork. Stir-fry until the pork changes color, about 3 to 5 minutes.

* Use butterfly pork chops, pork tenderloin, or boneless pork roast.

3. Return water chestnuts and cloud ears to the wok. Pour in sauce, stir a few seconds and serve.

Tip • This dish can be cooked a day ahead and refrigerated. Serve at room temperature or reheat in a microwave oven.

Braised Spareribs (Serves 2 to 3)　紅燒排骨

2 pounds pork spareribs*

Braising sauce:
½ teaspoon salt
2 tablespoons sugar
1 tablespoon dry sherry
¼ cup soy sauce
1 cup water

3 slices peeled ginger root
2 green onions, cut into 2-inch pieces
2 tablespoons oil

Garnish: cucumber pinwheels (page 176)

To Prepare Ahead:

1. With a cleaver or knife, separate the ribs by cutting between the bones. Trim off excess fat.

2. Combine sauce ingredients in a small mixing bowl.

To Cook:

1. Heat 2 tablespoons oil in a 6-quart saucepan over high heat. Add ginger root and green onions; then add the ribs, stirring for about 4 minutes.

2. Add sauce; when it comes to a boil, turn heat to medium. Cover and cook for 35 minutes, stirring 2 or 3 times. Adjust the cooking temperature so that the liquid does not boil away completely. There should be about ¼ cup of sauce left after 35 minutes. Discard the ginger root.

3. Skim the fat from the sauce. Garnish and serve.

Tips • This dish can be frozen. To reheat: place the spareribs in a saucepan over medium heat for 10 minutes adding some water if needed, or reheat in a microwave oven.

• When you double the recipe, double everything except the amount of water in the sauce.

* Ask the butcher to cut the ribs across the bones into 1½-inch strips.

Spareribs, Jing Tu Style (Serves 2)   京 都 排 骨

    1½ pounds pork spareribs*

Marinade for ribs:
    Dash freshly ground pepper
    ½ teaspoon salt
    2 teaspoons soy sauce
    2 teaspoons dry sherry

    1 tablespoon cornstarch

Seasoning sauce:
    1 tablespoon sugar
    2 tablespoons Worcestershire sauce
    1 tablespoon catsup
    1 tablespoon soy sauce
     or A1 Steak Sauce
    2 teaspoons cider vinegar
    2 tablespoons water
    1 teaspoon sesame oil
    3 cups oil for deep-frying

Garnish: sprigs of cilantro and lemon wedges

To Prepare Ahead:

1. With a cleaver or knife, separate the ribs by cutting between the bones. Trim off excess fat.

2. Transfer ribs to a large mixing bowl. Add marinade ingredients and toss to coat thoroughly. Let stand for 30 minutes.

3. Sprinkle cornstarch over the ribs and mix well.

4. Mix ingredients for seasoning sauce in a small bowl.

To Cook:

1. Heat 3 cups oil in a wok over high heat to 375°F. Add half the ribs and deep-fry for 5 minutes or until well done. Drain on paper towels.

2. Deep-fry the rest of the ribs.

3. Remove the hot oil to a heat-proof bowl and wipe the wok with a paper towel.

4. Add seasoning sauce to the wok and bring to a boil over medium heat. Add the deep-fried ribs. Stir constantly and cook until the liquid is absorbed. Garnish and serve.

Tip • This dish can be cooked a day in advance and refrigerated. Serve hot or at room temperature.

* Ask the butcher to cut the ribs across the bones into 1½-inch strips.

Stuffed Spareribs (Serves 2 to 3)　葱串排骨

      2 pounds pork spareribs*
      2 bunches green onions

   Braising sauce:
      ½ teaspoon salt
      2 tablespoons sugar
      1 tablespoon dry sherry
      ¼ cup soy sauce
      1 cup water

      2 tablespoons oil
      3 slices peeled ginger root
      1 teaspoon lemon juice
      ½ teaspoon sesame oil

To Prepare Ahead:

1. With a cleaver or knife, separate the ribs by cutting between the bones. Trim off excess fat.

2. Cut the white parts of green onions into 1½-inch pieces.

3. Mix sauce ingredients in a small bowl.

To Cook:

1. Heat 2 tablespoons oil in a 6-quart saucepan over high heat. Add ginger root; after a few seconds, add spareribs and cook for 4 minutes.

2. Add sauce and bring to a boil over high heat. Reduce heat to medium; cover and cook for 35 minutes, stirring 2 or 3 times. Adjust cooking temperature so that the liquid does not boil away completely. There should be about ¼ cup of sauce left after 35 minutes. Discard the ginger root.

3. Transfer the ribs to a plate, leaving the sauce in the saucepan. Skim fat from the sauce.

4. Remove the bone from each rib, and stuff with one piece of green onion (white portion only).

5. Return the ribs to the saucepan. Add lemon juice and cook over medium heat for 2 minutes, stirring occasionally. Add sesame oil. Mix and serve. (See picture on pages 26 and 27.)

Tips　• You can prepare this dish in advance through cooking step 4. Cool, cover, and refrigerate up to two days. Reheat in a saucepan over medium heat for 10 minutes, adding some water if needed, and proceed to step 5.

　　　　• When you double the recipe, double everything except the amount of water in the sauce.

* Ask the butcher to cut the ribs across the bones into 1½-inch strips.

Steamed Spareribs with Salted Black Beans (Serves 2)

1½ pounds pork spareribs*
1 tablespoon salted black beans

豉汁蒸排骨

Seasoning sauce:
   ½ teaspoon salt
   1 teaspoon sugar
   1 tablespoon dry sherry
   2 tablespoons soy sauce

1 tablespoon oil
2 teaspoons chopped garlic
¼ teaspoon minced ginger root
1 tablespoon cornstarch

To Prepare Ahead:

1. With a cleaver or knife, separate the ribs by cutting between the bones. Trim off excess fat.

2. Rinse salted black beans in a cup of water; drain and chop.

3. Mix ingredients for seasoning sauce in a small bowl.

To Cook:

1. In a steamer, bring 2 quarts of water to a boil over high heat.

2. Meanwhile, heat 1 tablespoon oil in a wok over medium heat. Add black beans, garlic, and ginger root; stir for a few seconds. (Be careful not to burn them.)

3. Add seasoning sauce and ribs to the wok; toss to coat.

4. Turn heat off. Sprinkle cornstarch over the ribs and mix well.

5. Place the ribs on a 10-inch heat-proof plate in a single layer.

6. Place the rib plate on a tier of the steamer and steam for 30 minutes. Serve with rice.

---

* Ask the butcher to cut the ribs across the bones into 1½-inch strips.

Poultry

Kung Pao Diced Chicken (Serves 3 to 4)　宮保鷄丁

1 pound chicken breast, boned and skinned*

Marinade for chicken:
    1 tablespoon cornstarch
    1 tablespoon soy sauce
    2 teaspoons dry sherry
    1 tablespoon water

½ cup shelled raw peanuts
2 dried red chili peppers

Seasoning sauce:
    1 teaspoon cornstarch
    1 teaspoon sugar
    ½ teaspoon salt
    2 teaspoons cider vinegar
    2 teaspoons dry sherry
    1 tablespoon soy sauce
    2 tablespoons water
    ½ teaspoon sesame oil

1 cup oil for deep-frying
3 tablespoons oil
2 slices peeled ginger root

To Prepare Ahead:

1. Dice chicken into ½-inch pieces.

2. Transfer chicken to a mixing bowl. Add marinade ingredients and toss to coat thoroughly. Let stand for 30 minutes or longer.

3. Pour 1 cup boiling water over peanuts and soak for a few minutes. Remove hulls and pat dry with a paper towel.

4. Cut each dried pepper crosswise into 3 pieces and remove seeds.

5. Mix ingredients for seasoning sauce in a small bowl.

To Cook:

1. Heat 1 cup oil in the wok over high heat to 325°F. Deep-fry peanuts for 1 to 2 minutes. Remove and drain on paper towels.

2. Heat 3 tablespoons oil in a wok over high heat. Add red peppers and cook until they are almost black. Add ginger root and chicken; stir-fry for 4 minutes. Discard the ginger root.

---

* See directions on page 115. You need almost 2 pounds of chicken breast with bone and skin to get 1 pound of meat.

3. Pour in seasoning sauce and stir for a few seconds. Transfer to a plate. Just before serving, top with peanuts.

Tip • This recipe can be served at room temperature or reheated in a microwave oven.

Lemon Chicken (Serves 3 to 4)　檸檬鷄片

1 pound chicken breast, boned and skinned*

Marinade for chicken:
　1 teaspoon salt
　2 teaspoons cornstarch
　2 teaspoons soy sauce
　2 teaspoons dry sherry
　2 egg yolks
　Dash white pepper

Batter:
　1 egg, beaten
　¼ cup cornstarch
　¼ cup flour
　¼ cup chicken broth

Lemon sauce:
　1 tablespoon cornstarch
　3 tablespoons sugar
　¼ cup water
　¼ cup fresh lemon juice
　⅓ cup chicken broth
　1 teaspoon sesame oil

3 cups oil for deep-frying

Garnish: lemon half, maraschino cherry, and fresh mint leaves

To Prepare Ahead:

1. Slant cleaver at a 45° angle to the cutting board and slice chicken across the grain into 1 x 2-inch pieces, ¼ inch thick.

2. Transfer chicken to a mixing bowl. Add marinade ingredients and toss to coat thoroughly. Let stand for 30 minutes or longer.

3. Mix batter ingredients in a bowl and blend until smooth.

4. Combine ingredients for lemon sauce in a small saucepan.

---

* See directions on page 115. You need almost 2 pounds of chicken breast with bone and skin to get 1 pound of meat.

To Cook:

1. Add chicken to batter and mix to coat well.

2. Heat 3 cups oil in a wok over high heat to 375°F. Add half the coated chicken pieces one by one. Deep-fry for 3 to 5 minutes. Transfer to a plate lined with paper towels.

3. Deep-fry rest of chicken the same way.

4. Bring sauce mixture to a boil over high heat, stirring occasionally.

5. Remove paper towels from chicken and pour sauce over it. Garnish and serve.

Moo Goo Gai Pan (Serves 2)　　蘑菇鷄片

½ pound chicken breast, boned and skinned*

Marinade for chicken:
　　2 teaspoons cornstarch
　　1 teaspoon dry sherry
　　2 teaspoons soy sauce
　　2 teaspoons water

4 ounces fresh snow peas *or* celery
4 ounces Chinese cabbage
4 ounces fresh mushrooms

Thickening sauce:
　　2 teaspoons cornstarch
　　2 teaspoons soy sauce
　　3 tablespoons water
　　½ teaspoon sesame oil

5 tablespoons oil
½ teaspoon salt
1 clove garlic, smashed and peeled
1 green onion, cut into 1½-inch pieces

To Prepare Ahead:

1. Slice chicken breast across the grain into pieces ⅛ inch thick.

2. Transfer chicken slices to a mixing bowl. Add marinade ingredients and toss to coat thoroughly. Let stand for 30 minutes or longer.

3. Wash snow peas and remove the tips and strings. (If using celery, cut diagonally into 2-inch pieces, ⅛ inch thick.)

* See directions on page 115. You need almost 1 pound of chicken breast with bone and skin to get ½ pound of meat.

4. Wash and drain Chinese cabbage. Cut crosswise into 1-inch pieces.

5. Rinse and slice mushrooms into ½-inch pieces.

6. Mix ingredients for thickening sauce in a small bowl.

To Cook:

1. Heat 1 tablespoon oil in a wok over high heat. Add snow peas, Chinese cabbage, and ¼ teaspoon salt. Stir-fry for 2 to 3 minutes. Transfer to a plate.

2. Wipe the wok with a paper towel and add 2 tablespoons oil. When hot, add mushrooms and ¼ teaspoon salt; stir-fry for 1 minute. Set aside with vegetables.

3. Rinse and dry the wok; pour in 2 tablespoons oil. When hot, add garlic, green onion, and chicken. Stir-fry until chicken turns white and firm, about 2 to 3 minutes. Discard the garlic.

4. Return vegetables to the wok and add sauce. Stir for a few seconds until thickened and serve. (See picture on jacket cover.)

Chicken with Cashews (Serves 3)　　腰果鷄丁

1 pound chicken breast*, boned and skinned**

Marinade for chicken:
    1 tablespoon cornstarch
    1 tablespoon soy sauce
    1 teaspoon dry sherry
    1 tablespoon water

10 water chestnuts
1 bell pepper

Seasoning sauce:
    ¼ teaspoon salt
    ½ teaspoon sugar
    1 teaspoon cornstarch
    1 teaspoon vinegar
    1 teaspoon dry sherry
    1 tablespoon soy sauce
    ½ teaspoon sesame oil
    3 tablespoons water

* You need almost 2 pounds of chicken breast with bone and skin to get 1 pound of meat.

4 tablespoons oil
¼ teaspoon salt
2 slices peeled ginger root
1 clove garlic, smashed and peeled
2 green onions, cut into ½-inch pieces
½ cup roasted cashews

To Prepare Ahead:

1. Cut chicken into ¾-inch cubes.

2. Transfer chicken cubes to a mixing bowl. Add marinade ingredients and toss to coat thoroughly. Let stand for 30 minutes or longer.

3. Quarter water chestnuts. Seed bell pepper and cut into ½-inch squares.

4. Mix ingredients for seasoning sauce in a small bowl.

To Cook:

1. Heat 1 tablespoon oil in a wok over high heat. Add bell pepper, water chestnuts, and ¼ teaspoon salt; stir-fry for 1 minute. Transfer to a plate.

2. Wipe the wok with a paper towel. Heat 3 tablespoons oil over high heat. Add ginger root and garlic; after a few seconds, add green onions and chicken. Stir-fry until the chicken turns white and firm, about 3 to 4 minutes. Discard ginger root and garlic.

3. Return vegetables to the wok and add sauce. Stir until thickened, top with cashews, and serve.

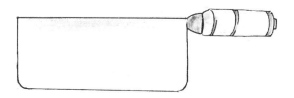

** To bone and skin a chicken breast:

1. Pull skin away from meat, using the cleaver as needed to free it.

2. Make 2 cuts along each side of the breastbone.

3. With your hands, pull the meat away from the ribs close to the bones, using the cleaver as needed.

4. Trim off fat and white tendons.

5. Repeat steps 3 and 4 with the other half.

Braised Chicken (Serves 4)   紅燒雞塊

    3 pounds chicken*

    Braising sauce:
        ½ teaspoon salt
        1 tablespoon rock sugar
            or brown sugar
        2 tablespoons dry sherry
        ⅓ cup soy sauce

    1 teaspoon cornstarch
    2 tablespoons oil
    3 slices peeled ginger root
    3 cloves garlic, smashed and peeled
    2 green onions, cut into 2-inch pieces

Garnish: 1 pound fresh spinach

To Prepare Ahead:

1. With a cleaver, chop chicken into 1-inch pieces across the bone.

2. Mix ingredients for braising sauce in a small bowl.

3. Mix cornstarch with 1 tablespoon water.

To Cook:

1. Heat 2 tablespoons oil in a wok over high heat. Add ginger root and garlic. After a few seconds, add green onions and chicken pieces. Stir occasionally for about 5 minutes.

2. Pour in braising sauce. Cover and cook over medium heat for 15 minutes, stirring twice.

3. Remove wok from the heat and skim off excess fat. Discard the ginger root and garlic. There should be about ½ cup sauce left.

4. Return wok to the burner. Stir in cornstarch mixture until sauce thickens.

5. Cook spinach and drain thoroughly (page 177). Place the cooked spinach on a serving plate and top with chicken and sauce.

Tip • You can cook this dish in advance through step 4 and either refrigerate or freeze. Reheat in a saucepan over medium-low heat for 10 to 15 minutes, adding more water if needed, or in a microwave oven.

* Drumsticks and thighs.

Smoked Chicken (Serves 4)   燻 鷄

> 1 (4-pound) chicken
> 2 teaspoons salt
> 1 teaspoon Szechwan peppercorns
> 3 slices peeled ginger root
> 2 tablespoons chopped green onion

> *Smoking agents:*
> ¾ cup sugar
> ½ cup flour
> ¼ cup tea leaves (any variety)

Garnish: tomato rose (page 175) and sprigs of cilantro

To Prepare the Day Before:

1. Rinse and drain the chicken; discard loose fat from the cavity. Blot dry.

2. In a small saucepan, roast salt and Szechwan peppercorns over medium heat for 2 minutes, stirring occasionally. Let cool.

3. Rub chicken with ginger root slices, then with chopped green onion.

4. Sprinkle salt and pepper mixture evenly over chicken, inside and out. Rub lightly.

5. Place ginger root and green onion inside cavity. Cover and refrigerate overnight or up to 2 days.

To Steam:

1. In a steamer bring 3 quarts of water to a boil over high heat. Place chicken in a heat-proof dish and steam for about 35 minutes.

2. Remove and drain well. Reserve the liquid for other use. Discard ginger root and green onion, brushing off peppercorns. Air-dry for 30 minutes. (This is important; any liquid dripping into smoking agents would decrease smoking efficiency.)

To Smoke:

You can use one of two methods.

A. **Indoor Method** - use a large old pot with a tight lid.

1. Line an old 6-quart pot with heavy duty aluminum foil. Sprinkle smoking agents evenly over the foil.

2. Place steamed chicken on a rack in the pot.

3. Cover pot tightly and place over medium heat. (Sugar will burn, creating smoke.) Smoke chicken for 15 minutes without opening. Turn off heat and keep pot closed for 30 minutes more.

4. Transfer chicken to a plate, cool, cover, and refrigerate for 4 hours or

overnight to mellow flavor.

B. **Outdoor Method** - use a covered barbecue grill.

1. Make a pan from a 14 x 18-inch sheet of heavy duty aluminum foil by folding edges up.

2. Sprinkle smoking agents evenly over foil pan and place it directly on the hot charcoal.

3. Put steamed chicken on the grill over the foil pan. Cover and smoke for 15 minutes or until golden brown.

4. Transfer chicken to a plate, cool, cover, and refrigerate for 4 hours or overnight to mellow flavor.

To Serve:

Either carve chicken American style (like carving a turkey), or Chinese style.* Garnish and serve.

Tips   • Serve as a main dish or as a cold plate at a banquet. (See picture on pages 18 and 19.) Leftover chicken is great for sandwiches. Remove the bones and mix meat with mayonnaise.

    • The liquid collected during steaming can be diluted and used as broth.

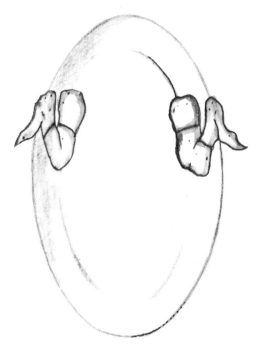

* **To chop and reassemble poultry:**

1. With a cleaver, disjoint wings and chop each into 3 pieces. Reassemble wings on each side of a platter.

2. Cut off legs through tendons at hip joints. Chop each into 1-inch pieces across the bone. Reassemble legs below the wings on each side of the platter.

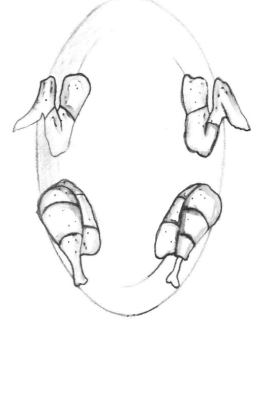

3. Split chicken in half lengthwise cutting through the breastbone and backbone sharply with the cleaver. Lay the back flat on the chopping board. Chop in half along the backbone, then crosswise into 1-inch pieces. Reassemble back pieces in the center of the platter between wings and legs.

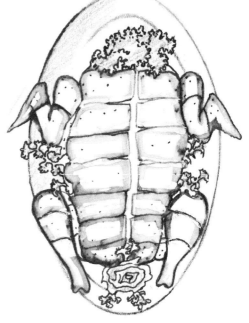

4. Chop breast in half along the breastbone, then crosswise into 1-inch pieces. Lay breast pieces on top of the back pieces. Garnish as desired.

Steamed Chicken (Serves 2) 蒸 鷄

    1½ pounds chicken thighs (about 6 thighs)
    3 thin slices peeled ginger root, shredded
    ½ teaspoon sugar
    ¾ teaspoon salt
    2 teaspoons cornstarch
    1 teaspoon soy sauce
    1 teaspoon oil
    1 teaspoon dry sherry
    Dash freshly ground pepper

Garnish: 1 tablespoon finely chopped green onion

To Prepare Ahead:

1. Rinse and trim fat from chicken thighs. Chop each thigh into 3 equal pieces across the bone.

2. In a large mixing bowl, mix chicken pieces with all ingredients except the garnish. Marinade for 30 minutes.

To Cook:

1. Arrange chicken pieces in a single layer on a heat-proof 10-inch plate.

2. In a steamer, bring 2 quarts of water to a brisk boil. Place plate of chicken on a tier. Cover and steam for 15 minutes over high heat.

3. Sprinkle with chopped green onion and serve.

Foil-Wrapped Chicken Slices (Serves 2) 錫 紙 包 鷄

    ½ pound chicken breast, boned and skinned*

Marinade for chicken:
    ¼ teaspoon salt
    2 teaspoons cornstarch
    2 teaspoons dry sherry
    ½ tablespoon soy sauce
    2 tablespoons oil
    Dash white pepper

    2 stalks celery
    ¼ teaspoon salt
    4 ounces cooked Virginia ham
      or other cooked ham
    ½ bunch cilantro (optional)
    1 tablespoon sesame oil
    15 pieces aluminum foil, each 6 x 6 inches

To Prepare Ahead:

1. Slant cleaver at a 45° angle to the cutting board, and slice the chicken across the grain into 1 x 2-inch pieces, ¼ inch thick.

2. Transfer chicken slices to a mixing bowl. Add marinade ingredients and toss to coat evenly.

3. Slant the cleaver at a 45° angle to the cutting board, and cut celery crosswise into ¼-inch slices.

4. Sprinkle celery with ¼ teaspoon salt and mix well. Add to chicken, mix again, and let stand for 30 minutes.

5. Slice ham into ½ x 2-inch pieces, ⅛ inch thick.

6. Remove root and stem of cilantro. Rinse in a pot of cold water and drain.

To Wrap:

1. Squirt 2 drops of sesame oil in the center of each aluminum foil square. Spread the oil into a 1-inch circle, using a pair of chopsticks or spoon.

2. Divide chicken, ham, celery, and cilantro among the pieces of foil. Fold as shown below:

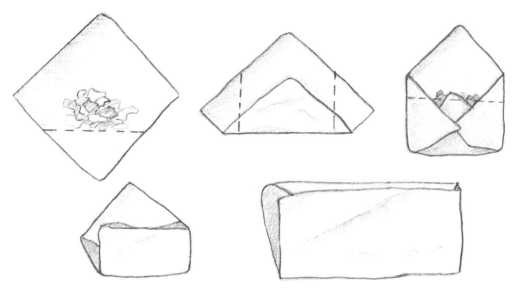

To Cook:

Preheat the oven to 450°F. Place envelopes of chicken on a cookie sheet and bake for 15 minutes.

To Serve:

Unwrap with fingers. Serve with rice.

---

* See directions on page 115. You need almost 1 pound of chicken breast with bone and skin to get ½ pound of meat.

Soy Sauce Chicken (Serves 4)　醬　油　鷄

1 (3-pound) chicken

Cooking sauce:
   ½ teaspoon salt
   ¼ cup rock sugar
      or brown sugar
   ¼ cup dry sherry
   1 cup soy sauce
   1 cup water
   2 green onions, cut into 2-inch pieces
   2 slices peeled ginger root
   2 whole star anise
      or an equal amount of broken pieces

   1 tablespoon sesame oil

Garnish: shredded green onion and pineapple "bow ties" (page 176)

1. Rinse and drain chicken. Remove loose fat from the cavity. Scald chicken by pouring 2 quarts boiling water over it; drain and discard water.

2. Combine ingredients for cooking sauce in a 4-quart saucepan and bring to a boil over high heat. Add the chicken, breast side up. Bring to a boil, reduce heat to medium-low, cover, and simmer for 10 minutes.

3. Turn the chicken over carefully and simmer for 15 minutes more. Check for doneness by poking a chopstick or fork into the thigh; there should be no pink juice seeping out.

4. Turn heat off, cover and let chicken steep in the sauce for 1 hour.

5. Remove chicken and brush with 2 teaspoons sesame oil.

6. Strain sauce through a fine sieve; skim off fat.

7. Chop and reassemble chicken as shown on pages 118 and 119.

8. Mix 1 teaspoon sesame oil with ¼ cup sauce; pour over the chopped chicken pieces. Garnish and serve.

Tips
- This dish can be cooked a day ahead through step 6. Refrigerate the chicken and sauce separately overnight. Before serving, do steps 7 and 8. Serve cold.

- The leftover sauce can be frozen and reused by adding a little more seasoning and spices each time.

Stir-Fried Chicken with Broccoli (Serves 2)　　玉蘭鷄片

½ pound chicken breast, boned and skinned*

Marinade for chicken:
   2 teaspoons cornstarch
   2 teaspoons soy sauce
   1 teaspoon dry sherry
   2 teaspoons water

1 pound fresh broccoli

Thickening sauce:
   2 teaspoons cornstarch
   2 teaspoons soy sauce
   4 tablespoons water
   ¼ teaspoon sesame oil

5 tablespoons oil
¾ teaspoon salt
1 clove garlic, smashed and peeled
1 green onion, cut into 1½-inch pieces

To Prepare Ahead:

1. Slice chicken across the grain into pieces ⅛ inch thick.

2. Transfer chicken slices to a mixing bowl. Add marinade ingredients and toss to coat thoroughly. Let stand for 30 minutes or longer.

3. Wash and drain broccoli. Peel tough skin from the bottom of the stems with a paring knife. Cut each stalk into 3 or 4 equal sections. Slice stem sections lengthwise into ¼-inch pieces. Separate the flowerets into bite-sized pieces.

4. Mix ingredients for thickening sauce in a small bowl.

To Cook:

1. Heat 2 tablespoons oil in a wok over high heat. Add broccoli and salt, and stir-fry for 3 minutes. (Add 1 tablespoon water if it gets too dry.) Transfer to a plate.

2. Wipe the wok with a paper towel and pour in 3 tablespoons oil. When hot, add garlic, green onion, and chicken mixture. Stir-fry until chicken turns white and firm, about 2 to 3 minutes. Discard the garlic.

3. Return broccoli to the wok and add sauce. Stir until thickened and serve.

---

* See directions on page 115. You need almost 1 pound of chicken breast with bone and skin to get ½ pound of meat.

Stir-Fried Chicken with Cauliflower (Serves 2) 菜花鷄片

½ pound chicken breast, boned and skinned*

Marinade for chicken:
    2 teaspoons cornstarch
    2 teaspoons soy sauce
    1 teaspoon dry sherry
    2 teaspoons water

1 small head cauliflower, about 1 pound

Thickening sauce:
    1 teaspoon cornstarch
    1 teaspoon soy sauce
    2 tablespoons water
      or chicken broth

5 tablespoons oil
¾ teaspoon salt
¼ cup chicken broth
1 clove garlic, smashed and peeled
1 green onion, cut into 1½-inch pieces

To Prepare Ahead:

1. Slice chicken across the grain into pieces ⅛ inch thick.

2. Transfer chicken slices to a mixing bowl. Add marinade ingredients and toss to coat thoroughly. Let stand for 30 minutes or longer.

3. Wash cauliflower and separate into bite-sized flowerets.

4. Mix ingredients for thickening sauce in a small bowl.

To Cook:

1. Heat 2 tablespoons oil in a wok over high heat. Add cauliflower and salt, and stir for 1 minute. Pour in ¼ cup chicken broth, cover, and cook over medium-high heat for 2 minutes. Transfer to a plate.

2. Wipe the wok with a paper towel and add 3 tablespoons oil. When hot, add garlic, green onion, and chicken mixture. Stir-fry until chicken turns white and firm, about 2 to 3 minutes. Discard the garlic.

3. Return cauliflower to the wok and add sauce. Stir until thickened and serve.

---

* See directions on page 115. You need almost 1 pound of chicken breast with bone and skin to get ½ pound of meat.

Stir-Fried Chicken with Chinese Cabbage (Serves 2) 白菜鷄片

½ pound chicken breast, boned and skinned*

Marinade for chicken:
2 teaspoons cornstarch
2 teaspoons soy sauce
1 teaspoon dry sherry
2 teaspoons water

1 pound Chinese cabbage

Thickening sauce:
2 teaspoons cornstarch
1 teaspoon soy sauce
2 tablespoons water
¼ teaspoon sesame oil

5 tablespoons oil
¾ teaspoon salt
1 clove garlic, smashed and peeled
1 green onion, cut into 1½-inch pieces

To Prepare Ahead:

1. Slice chicken across the grain into pieces ⅛ inch thick.

2. Transfer chicken slices to a mixing bowl. Add marinade ingredients and toss to coat thoroughly. Let stand for 30 minutes or longer.

3. Wash and drain Chinese cabbage. Cut crosswise into ½-inch pieces.

4. Mix ingredients for thickening sauce in a small bowl.

To Cook:

1. Heat 2 tablespoons oil in wok over high heat. Add Chinese cabbage and salt, and stir-fry for 3 to 4 minutes. Transfer to a plate.

2. Wipe the wok with a paper towel and pour in 3 tablespoons oil. When hot, add garlic, green onion, and chicken mixture. Stir-fry until the chicken turns white and firm, about 2 to 3 minutes. Discard the garlic.

3. Return cabbage to the wok and add sauce. Stir until thickened and serve.

* See directions on page 115. You need almost 1 pound of chicken breast with bone and skin to get ½ pound of meat.

Stir-Fried Chicken with Zucchini (Serves 2)

½ pound chicken breast, boned and skinned*

Marinade for chicken:
    2 teaspoons cornstarch
    2 teaspoons soy sauce
    1 teaspoon dry sherry
    2 teaspoons water

1 pound fresh zucchini, about 2 to 3

Thickening sauce:
    1 teaspoon cornstarch
    2 teaspoons soy sauce
    3 tablespoons water

5 tablespoons oil
¾ teaspoon salt
1 clove garlic, smashed and peeled
1 green onion, cut into 1½-inch pieces

To Prepare Ahead:

1. Slice chicken across the grain into pieces ⅛ inch thick.

2. Transfer chicken slices to a mixing bowl. Add marinade ingredients and toss to coat thoroughly. Let stand for 30 minutes or longer.

3. Wash zucchini and remove ends. Cut in half lengthwise; then cut diagonally into pieces 1½ inches long, and ⅛ inch thick.

4. Mix ingredients for thickening sauce in a small bowl.

To Cook:

1. Heat 2 tablespoons oil in a wok over high heat. Add zucchini slices and salt, and stir-fry for 2 to 3 minutes. (Add 1 tablespoon water if it gets too dry.) Transfer to a plate.

2. Wipe the wok with a paper towel and add 3 tablespoons oil. When hot, add garlic, green onion, and chicken mixture. Stir-fry until chicken turns white and firm, about 2 to 3 minutes. Discard the garlic.

3. Return zucchini to the wok and pour in sauce. Stir until thickened and serve.

---

* See directions on page 115. You need almost 1 pound of chicken breast with bone and skin to get ½ pound of meat.

Stir-Fried Diced Chicken (Serves 2)   生炒鷄丁

½ pound chicken breast, boned and skinned*

Marinade for chicken:
2 teaspoons cornstarch
2 teaspoons soy sauce
1 teaspoon dry sherry
2 teaspoons water
¼ teaspoon minced garlic
1 tablespoon chopped green onion

6 Chinese dried mushrooms
½ cup diced cooked ham
½ cup diced bamboo shoots
½ cup diced water chestnuts

Thickening sauce:
2 teaspoons cornstarch
2 teaspoons soy sauce
½ cup chicken broth
1 teaspoon sesame oil
Dash freshly ground pepper

4 tablespoons oil
½ cup green peas, fresh or frozen
½ teaspoon salt

To Prepare Ahead:

1. Partially freeze chicken breast for easy dicing. Dice into ¼-inch pieces.

2. Transfer chicken to a mixing bowl. Add marinade ingredients and toss to coat thoroughly. Let stand for 30 minutes or longer.

3. Soak mushrooms in 2 cups hot water for 20 minutes. Rinse, squeeze dry and discard stems. Dice caps into ¼-inch pieces.

4. Mix ingredients for thickening sauce in a small bowl.

To Cook:

1. Heat 2 tablespoons oil in a wok over high heat. Add mushrooms, ham, bamboo shoots, water chestnuts, green peas, and salt. Stir-fry for 2 minutes. Transfer to a plate.

2. Rinse and dry the wok. Add 2 tablespoons oil. When hot, add chicken and stir-fry for 2 minutes.

3. Return ham and vegetables to the wok and pour in sauce. Stir until thickened.

* See directions on page 115. You need almost 1 pound of chicken breast with bone and skin to get ½ pound of meat.

To Serve: Serve one of three ways:

1. Serve as a regular dish with rice.

2. Serve with whole lettuce leaves. Place about 2 tablespoons of chicken mixture on the leaf; wrap with your fingers and eat.

3. Serve with **Mandarin Pancakes** (page 168). Place about 2 tablespoons of chicken mixture on each pancake; wrap with your fingers and eat.

Sweet and Sour Chicken (Serves 3 to 4)　糖　醋　鷄

    1 pound chicken breast, boned and skinned*
    1½ teaspoons salt
    1 tablespoon soy sauce
    1 bell pepper
    4 canned pineapple rings
    6 cherry tomatoes
     or one medium tomato

Batter:
    1 egg, lightly beaten
    ¼ cup cornstarch
    ¼ cup flour
    ¼ cup chicken broth

Sweet and sour sauce:
    2 tablespoons sugar
    1 tablespoon cornstarch
    2 tablespoons water
    3 tablespoons white vinegar
    3 tablespoons catsup
    1 teaspoon soy sauce
    ¼ teaspoon sesame oil
    ⅓ cup pineapple juice
    ⅓ cup chicken broth

    3 cups oil for deep-frying
    1 tablespoon oil

To Prepare Ahead:

1. Cut chicken into 1-inch cubes.

2. Transfer chicken to a mixing bowl. Add 1 teaspoon salt and 1 tablespoon soy sauce; mix well.

---

* See directions on page 115. You need almost 2 pounds chicken breast with bone and skin to get 1 pound of meat.

3. Seed bell pepper and cut into 1-inch squares. Drain the pineapple, reserving the juice. Cut each slice into 8 pieces. Cut cherry tomatoes in half or tomato into ½-inch dice.

4. Mix batter ingredients in a mixing bowl until well blended.

5. Mix ingredients for sweet and sour sauce in a small saucepan.

To Cook:

1. Add chicken cubes to the batter and mix well.

2. Heat 3 cups oil in a wok over high heat to 375°F. Or you can test the oil by adding a drop of batter to the hot oil. If the batter comes to the surface immediately, the oil is hot enough.

3. Add half the coated chicken cubes, one by one, to the hot oil. Deep-fry for 5 minutes, or until golden brown and fully cooked.

4. With a strainer, transfer chicken to a platter lined with paper towels.

5. Deep-fry the rest of chicken cubes.

6. Transfer the oil to a heat-proof bowl. Wipe the wok with a paper towel.

7. Bring the sweet and sour sauce to a boil over high heat, stirring occasionally. Cover and remove from heat.

8. Heat 1 tablespoon oil in the wok over high heat. Add bell pepper and ½ teaspoon salt, and stir-fry for 1 minute. Add pineapple, tomato, and sauce; bring to a boil.

9. Remove paper towels from chicken. Pour the sauce mixture over it and serve.

Tip • The chicken can be fried ahead and frozen for future use. When ready to use, place chicken on a cookie sheet and bake at 350°F. for 10 minutes. Proceed to steps 7, 8, and 9.

White-Cut Chicken (Serves 4)　白 切 鷄

> 1 (4-pound) chicken
> 3 slices peeled ginger root
> 40 ice cubes
>
> *Dipping sauce:*
> > ¼ teaspoon spiced ginger powder
> > 2 teaspoons minced ginger root
> > 2 tablespoons finely chopped whites of green onion
> > 2 tablespoons oil
> > 2 tablespoons oyster sauce
> > ¼ cup soy sauce

Garnish: shredded green onions

The Day Before:

1. Rinse and drain the chicken; discard the fat from the cavity.

2. Place chicken in a heavy 6-quart saucepan. Add enough cold water to the pan to cover the chicken.

3. Remove the chicken and bring the water to a brisk boil. Carefully add chicken, breast side down, and ginger root slices.

4. Bring to a boil, reduce heat to medium-low (just enough to keep water bubbling slightly), cover, and simmer for 25 minutes. Check for doneness by poking a chopstick or fork into the thigh; there should be no pink juice seeping out.

5. Turn heat off, leave covered, and let chicken steep for an hour. Do not peek.

6. Fill a 6-quart pot ⅔ full with cold water. Add 40 ice cubes.

7. Plunge chicken into the ice water for 5 minutes.(This tightens the chicken skin, giving it a very nice texture.)

8. Drain, cover, and refrigerate overnight.

To Prepare Dipping Sauce:

1. Put spiced ginger powder, minced ginger root, and green onion in a small heat-proof bowl.

2. Heat oil in a small saucepan until smoking. Pour the hot oil into the bowl.

3. Add oyster sauce and soy sauce to the bowl and mix well.

To Serve:

Chop and reassemble chicken on a platter as shown on pages 118 and 119. Garnish and serve with dipping sauce.

Tip • This dish should be served cold as a main dish or as part of a Chinese cold plate.

Beer Duck (Serves 4) 啤 酒 鴨

1 (5-pound) duck

Cooking sauce:
   1 teaspoon salt
   3 tablespoons rock sugar
     or brown sugar
   15 Szechwan peppercorns
   3 whole star anise
     or an equal amount of broken pieces
   3 slices peeled ginger root
   3 green onions
   ½ cup soy sauce
   1 can beer

1 teaspoon sesame oil
6 green onions, cut into 2-inch pieces

1. Thaw duck completely. Rinse and drain the duck; discard loose fat from the cavity. Scald by pouring 2 quarts of boiling water over it; drain and discard water.

2. Combine ingredients for cooking sauce in a 6-quart saucepan and bring to a boil over high heat. Add the duck. Cover and cook over medium-low heat for 1½ hours, turning the duck a couple of times during cooking.

3. Transfer duck from the pan to a platter. Skim off fat and strain the sauce. There should be about ½ cup of sauce.

4. Return sauce to the saucepan, and add sesame oil and green onion pieces. Bring to a boil and pour over the duck. Serve.

Tip • If desired, you can prepare the dish through step 3; refrigerate the duck and sauce separately overnight. Before serving, chop and reassemble duck as shown on pages 118 -119 and do step 4.

Crisp Duck with Eight-Treasure Stuffing (Serves 4 to 6)

1 (5-pound) duck
1 tablespoon salt
½ teaspoon freshly ground pepper
1 cup sweet rice
1¼ cups water

脆皮八寶鴨

Stuffing ingredients:
   2 tablespoons oil
   1 green onion, chopped
Eight treasures:
   1 duck gizzard, cut into ¼-inch dice
   4 Chinese dried mushrooms, soaked and diced
   ¼ cup diced water chestnuts
   ¼ cup diced bamboo shoots
   ¼ cup canned gingko nuts
   ¼ cup dried lotus seeds, soaked and drained
   ½ cup diced cooked Virginia ham
     or other cooked ham
   1 tablespoon dried shrimp, soaked and chopped coarsely
  Dash freshly ground pepper
  ½ teaspoon salt
  1 tablespoon dry sherry
  1 tablespoon soy sauce

2 tablespoons soy sauce
1 teaspoon five-spice powder
3 tablespoons flour
4 cups oil for deep-frying

Garnish: sprigs of cilantro and pineapple "flowers" (page 176)

To Bone Duck: (Important: try to keep the skin intact.)

1. Thaw duck completely. Remove loose fat from the cavity. Rinse and drain.

2. Fold the neck skin back. With a sharp knife and poultry shears, loosen meat and skin from carcass by making tiny cuts against the bones.

3. Locate the joints that connect the wings to the carcass. Cut through joints to detach the wings.

4. Continue to fold meat and skin back, and free from carcass by making tiny cuts close to the bones. Pull meat and skin back, exposing more and more carcass.

5. When you have loosened the meat down to the thighs, free meat from the thighs and disjoin thigh bones from drumsticks, leaving drumsticks intact.

6. Cut and scrape meat away from bones all the way to the tail. Cut around the opening of the body cavity, leaving the tail intact. Remove carcass.

7. Turn the duck right side out and you have a whole boned duck (only the wing and drumstick bones remain intact).

8. Sprinkle 1 tablespoon salt and ½ teaspoon pepper over duck inside and out.

To Boil Sweet Rice:

1. In a small saucepan, rinse and drain rice. Add 1¼ cups water.

2. Bring to a boil over high heat. Turn heat to medium, cover the pan halfway and boil for 5 minutes.

3. Turn heat to low, cover, and simmer for 10 minutes.

4. Turn heat off and let stand for 10 minutes more.

To Make Stuffing:

1. Heat 2 tablespoons oil in a wok over high heat. Add chopped green onion, gizzard, and mushrooms; stir for 1 minute.

2. Add water chestnuts, bamboo shoots, gingko nuts, lotus seeds, ham, and shrimp; stir for 1 minute.

3. Add dash pepper, ½ teaspoon salt, 1 tablespoon dry sherry, and 1 tablespoon soy sauce. Mix thoroughly.

4. Remove from heat and add cooked sweet rice. Mix well.

To Stuff Duck:

1. Close neck cavity securely with stainless skewers or by sewing. Scoop stuffing into the body cavity.

2. Close body cavity with more skewers.

To Steam:

1. Bring 3 quarts water to a boil over high heat in a steamer.

2. Place duck, breast-side up, in a large heat-proof bowl. Steam over high heat for 1½ hours, replenishing water as needed.

3. Remove and drain duck.

4. Brush duck with 2 tablespoons soy sauce and sprinkle with 1 teaspoon five-spice powder.

To Deep-Fry:

1. Dust the duck with 3 tablespoons flour.

2. Heat 4 cups oil in a wok over high heat to 375°F. Deep-fry the duck until golden brown.

3. Remove and drain on paper towels.

To Serve:

1. Transfer duck to a platter.

2. Remove skewers, and cut duck lengthwise into 3 parts, then crosswise at 1-inch intervals. Garnish and serve.

Tips
- This is a rather complicated dish, but you can do most of the preparation in advance, or even a day before. Deep-fry 1 hour before serving and keep warm in the oven. Cut just before serving.

- You can omit some of the "treasures" or substitute other ingredients. It is not necessary to have exactly eight different things.

- The liquid collected in the large heat-proof bowl during steaming can be used as broth after fat is skimmed off. You can also use the neck, liver, carcass, and thigh bones for broth. (Simmer with 1 slice ginger root in 2 cups water for 1½ hours, and salt to taste.)

Roast Duck (Serves 4)   烤 鴨

1 (5-pound) duck

Mixture (I):
4 tablespoons honey
1 tablespoon vinegar
1 quart water

1 tablespoon salt
¼ teaspoon freshly ground pepper

Mixture (II):
3 slices peeled ginger root
1 green onion, cut into 2-inch pieces
¼ teaspoon five-spice powder
1 tablespoon dry sherry
2 tablespoons soy sauce
2 tablespoons bean sauce
1 whole star anise
or an equal amount of broken pieces

plum sauce (optional)

Garnish: green onion brushes (page 175)

To Prepare the Day Before:

1. Thaw duck completely. Remove loose fat from the cavity. Rinse and drain.

2. In a saucepan, bring mixture (I) to a boil over high heat. Place duck in a large mixing bowl and pour mixture (I) over it. Discard the liquid. Drain duck.

3. Sprinkle salt and pepper over duck, inside and out.

4. Tie a string around the neck skin. Hang duck up for 2 hours, using a dish to catch the drippings.

5. Place duck on a large platter and refrigerate uncovered overnight.

To Cook:

1. Preheat oven to 350°F. Combine mixture (II) in a bowl.

2. Close the neck cavity with 6-inch stainless skewers. Pour mixture (II) into the body cavity and close with skewers.

3. Wrap wings loosely with aluminum foil. Place duck, breast side down, on a rack in a roasting pan lined with aluminum foil. Roast for 45 minutes.

4. Carefully turn duck breast side up, trying not to break the skin. Remove foil from the wings. Roast for another 45 minutes or until golden brown.

5. Transfer duck to a serving platter. Discard fat in the roasting pan. Let duck stand for 5 minutes.

6. Remove skewers. Pour sauce from inside the duck through a strainer. Discard ingredients that do not pass through the strainer.

7. Chop and reassemble duck on a platter as shown on pages 118 and 119. Pour sauce over duck. Garnish and serve with or without plum sauce.

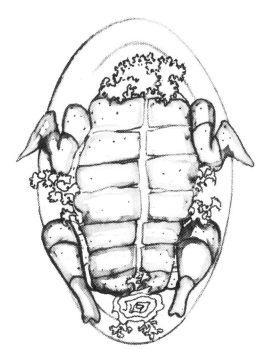

Szechwan Crisp Duck (Serves 4)　香 酥 鴨

>   1 (5-pound) duck
>   1 tablespoon salt
>   1 teaspoon Szechwan peppercorns
>   5 slices peeled ginger root
>   1 teaspoon five-spice powder
>   2 tablespoons soy sauce
>   3 tablespoons flour
>   4 cups oil for deep-frying

Garnish: carrot roses (page 177) and sprigs of cilantro

To Prepare the Day Before:

1. Thaw duck completely. Remove loose fat from the cavity. Rinse duck and dry with paper towels.

2. In a small saucepan, roast salt and Szechwan peppercorns over medium heat for 2 minutes, stirring occasionally. Let cool and crush with the handle of a cleaver.

3. Rub duck inside and out with ginger root and roasted salt-pepper mixture. Cover and refrigerate overnight.

To Cook:

1. Bring 3 quarts water to a brisk boil in a steamer.

2. Drain liquid off the duck. Place duck in a large heat-proof bowl and steam over high heat for 2 hours, replenishing water as needed.

3. Transfer duck to a platter and air-dry for 30 minutes. Discard the ginger root.

4. Rub five-spice powder and soy sauce over the duck. Sprinkle with flour.

5. Heat 4 cups oil in the wok over high heat to 375°F. Lower duck carefully into the hot oil; deep-fry about 15 minutes or until crisp and golden brown. Drain and transfer to a platter.

To Serve:

Garnish and serve with **Steamed Flower Rolls** (page 168) and roasted salt-Szechwan pepper (page 47).

Tip　• The liquid collected in the heat-proof bowl during steaming can be used as broth after the fat is skimmed off.

Seafood

Abalone with Chinese Cabbage (Serves 2 to 3)   鮑魚燴白菜

    1 (1-pound) can abalone
    2 pounds Chinese cabbage

Thickening sauce:
    1 tablespoon cornstarch
    1 tablespoon water
    ⅓ cup abalone juice

    4 tablespoons oil
    1 teaspoon salt

To Prepare Ahead:

1. Drain abalone, reserving juice. Slice ⅛ inch thick.

2. Wash, drain, and cut Chinese cabbage crosswise into 1-inch pieces.

3. Mix ingredients for thickening sauce in a small bowl.

To Cook:

1. Heat 4 tablespoons oil in a wok over high heat. Add Chinese cabbage and salt, stirring occasionally for 3 minutes. Cover and cook for 5 minutes. Discard liquid.

2. Pour in sauce, stir, and bring to a boil; then turn heat off.

3. With a large slotted spoon, transfer cabbage to a serving dish, leaving sauce in the wok.

4. Turn heat to medium. Add abalone slices, stirring to coat with sauce (about 30 seconds). Pour over Chinese cabbage and serve.

Tip   • Canned abalone can be served without cooking as part of a Chinese cold plate. (See picture on pages 18 and 19.)

Crabmeat with Chinese Cabbage (Serves 2) 蟹肉白菜

        6 ounces frozen crabmeat
          or Alaska King crabmeat
        2 pounds Chinese cabbage

    Cornstarch mixture:
        1½ tablespoons cornstarch
        1 tablespoon water

        4 tablespoons oil
        ¼ cup chicken broth
        1 teaspoon salt
        Dash white pepper
        1 teaspoon sesame oil

To Prepare Ahead:

1. Thaw crabmeat completely.

2. Wash, drain, and cut Chinese cabbage crosswise into 1-inch pieces.

3. Mix cornstarch with water in a small bowl.

To Cook:

1. Heat 4 tablespoons oil in a wok over high heat. Add Chinese cabbage, stirring occasionally for 3 minutes. Cover and cook for 5 minutes. Discard liquid.

2. Add chicken broth, salt, and crabmeat, stirring gently until it comes to a boil.

3. Add cornstarch mixture, white pepper, and sesame oil. Stir until thickened and serve.

Lobster Cantonese (Serves 2)   粵式龍蝦

    1 live lobster, about 2 pounds
    1 tablespoon salted black beans
    2 cloves garlic, smashed and peeled

Sauce:
    ¼ teaspoon sugar
    1 teaspoon salt
    1 teaspoon lemon juice
    1 tablespoon dry sherry
    1 tablespoon soy sauce
    ½ cup chicken broth
    Dash freshly ground pepper

Cornstarch mixture:
    2 teaspoons cornstarch
    2 tablespoons water

    3 tablespoons oil
    ½ teaspoon minced ginger root
    ¼ pound lean ground pork
    1 egg
    2 green onions, finely chopped

To Prepare Ahead:

1. Plunge live lobster into a large pot of boiling water for a few seconds and take it out.

2. Twist off large claws and legs. Crack claws with a hammer and chop into 1-inch pieces. Discard the end joints of legs, except the sections that are connected to the body.

3. Remove shell from head. Discard stomach sac and the spongy substance (lungs), but keep the greenish tomalley (liver) and red roe, if there is any.

4. With a cleaver, chop off the tip of the head where the antennae and eyes are located. Separate the head from the tail, and chop tail into sections.

5. Cut head into pieces about 1 x 1-inch square. Cut each tail section in half lengthwise.

6. Rinse and drain salted black beans. Combine beans with garlic in a rice bowl and mash with the handle of a cleaver.

7. Mix sauce ingredients in a bowl.

8. Mix cornstarch and water in another bowl.

To Cook:

1. Heat 3 tablespoons oil in a wok over high heat. Add ginger root, black

beans, garlic, pork, tomalley, and roe. Stir quickly for 1 to 2 minutes.

2. Add lobster and stir for 1 minute. Pour in sauce and bring to a boil over high heat. Turn heat to low, cover, and simmer for 5 minutes.

3. Return heat to high. Add cornstarch mixture, stirring until it bubbles.

4. Add egg, stir slowly for a few seconds. Transfer to a platter and sprinkle with chopped green onions. Serve hot with rice.

Spicy Scallops with Straw Mushrooms (Serves 2 to 3) 草菇鮮干貝

1 pound fresh scallops
1 (8-ounce) can straw mushrooms
15 water chestnuts

Sauce:
½ teaspoon sugar
1 tablespoon cornstarch
1 tablespoon chicken broth
1 tablespoon dry sherry
1½ tablespoons hot bean sauce
2 tablespoons oyster sauce
1 tablespoon soy sauce

4 tablespoons oil
½ teaspoon salt
4 slices peeled ginger root
3 green onions, chopped

To Prepare Ahead:

1. Rinse and drain scallops. Slice crosswise ¼ inch thick.

2. Drain straw mushrooms and water chestnuts. Cut each water chestnut into 3 circles.

3. Mix sauce ingredients in a small bowl.

To Cook:

1. Heat 2 tablespoons oil in a wok over high heat. Add mushrooms, water chestnuts, and salt; and stir-fry for 3 minutes. Transfer to a plate.

2. Rinse and dry the wok, and pour in 2 tablespoons oil. When hot, add ginger root, then scallops. Stir-fry for 3 minutes. Discard the ginger root.

3. Add chopped green onions, sauce, water chestnuts, and mushrooms. Stir until thickened and serve.

Braised Whole Fish (Serves 2 to 3)　　紅燒全魚

　　1 (1½-pound) fresh trout
　　　or red snapper, bass, flounder
　　1 teaspoon salt
　　4 ounces lean pork

　　Marinade for pork:
　　　1 teaspoon cornstarch
　　　1 teaspoon dry sherry
　　　2 teaspoons soy sauce
　　　2 thin slices peeled ginger root, shredded

　　4 Chinese dried mushrooms

　　Braising sauce:
　　　Dash freshly ground pepper
　　　2 teaspoons sugar
　　　1 teaspoon lemon juice
　　　2 tablespoons dry sherry
　　　3 tablespoons soy sauce
　　　¾ cup chicken broth

　　2 tablespoons cornstarch
　　7 tablespoons oil
　　¼ cup shredded bamboo shoots
　　4 slices peeled ginger root
　　2 cloves garlic, smashed and peeled
　　5 green onions, shredded

To Prepare Ahead:

1. Scale and clean fish; rinse under cold water and pat dry with paper towels. Score fish by making cuts ¼ inch deep at 2-inch intervals on both sides. (Cut fish in half if too long to fit in wok.)

2. Sprinkle salt evenly over fish, inside and out, and refrigerate for 30 minutes.

3. Shred pork by slicing it ⅛ inch thick across the grain; then cut the slices into strips about ⅛ x ⅛ x 1½ inches.

4. Transfer pork shreds to a mixing bowl. Add marinade ingredients and toss to coat evenly. Let stand for 30 minutes.

5. Soak dried mushrooms in a cup of hot water for 20 minutes. Rinse and squeeze dry. Cut off stems and shred caps into strips.

6. Mix ingredients for braising sauce in a bowl.

7. Before pan-frying, sprinkle 2 tablespoons cornstarch on both sides of fish.

To Cook:

1. Heat 2 tablespoons oil in a wok over high heat. Add pork and mushrooms, and stir-fry for 2 minutes. Add bamboo shoots, stirring for 1 minute more. Transfer to a plate.

2. Rinse and dry the wok. Pour in 5 tablespoons oil and swirl. Add 4 slices ginger root and garlic; a few seconds later, add fish. Reduce heat to medium and pan-fry for about 5 minutes or until golden brown. Turn fish over, trying not to break the skin, and brown 5 minutes more. Discard the ginger root and garlic.

3. Pour in braising sauce, cover, and simmer for 3 minutes. Turn fish over and add pork, mushrooms, and bamboo shoots to the wok. Cover and simmer for 3 minutes more. There should be about ½ cup sauce left.

4. Carefully remove fish to an oval platter, leaving the sauce and other ingredients in the wok. (If you cut the fish in half, put the halves back together like a whole fish.) Add green onions to the wok and heat until bubbling. Pour the contents over the fish and serve.

Steamed Fish (Serves 2)　清 蒸 魚

    1 (1½-pound) **very fresh** red snapper *or* trout
    1 teaspoon salt
    3 thin slices peeled ginger root
    3 green onions, shredded
    2 tablespoons soy sauce
    4 tablespoons oil

To Prepare Ahead:

1. Scale and clean fish; rinse under cold water and pat dry with paper towels.

2. Score fish by making cuts ¼ inch deep at 2-inch intervals on both sides. (Cut fish in half if too long to fit in plate.)

3. Sprinkle fish with salt inside and out. Place on a heat-proof plate.

4. Shred ginger root and spread evenly over fish. Refrigerate for 30 minutes or longer.

To Cook:

1. Bring 2 quarts of water to a boil in a steamer over high heat. Place plate of fish on a tier. Cover and steam for 12 to 15 minutes.

2. Transfer fish to a warm oval platter. (If you cut the fish in half, put the halves back together like a whole fish.)

3. Spread green onions and sprinkle soy sauce evenly over the fish.

4. In a small saucepan, heat 4 tablespoons oil to the smoking point over high heat. Pour oil over fish and serve.

Sliced Fish with Salted Black Beans (Serves 2 to 3)   豆豉魚片

1 pound fresh trout fillets

Marinade for fish:
    1 teaspoon cornstarch
    ½ teaspoon salt
    1 teaspoon lemon juice
    1 teaspoon oil
    2 teaspoons dry sherry
    Dash white pepper

4 ounces fresh snow peas
1 teaspoon chopped garlic
2 teaspoons salted black beans

Thickening sauce:
    2 teaspoons cornstarch
    1 teaspoon soy sauce
    ¼ teaspoon sesame oil
    ½ cup chicken broth

3½ tablespoons oil
½ teaspoon salt
4 slices peeled ginger root
2 green onions, chopped

To Prepare Ahead:

1. Cut fish fillets crosswise into ¼-inch slices.

2. Transfer fish slices to a mixing bowl. Add marinade ingredients and mix well. Refrigerate for 30 minutes or longer.

3. Rinse snow peas and remove the tips and strings.

4. Rinse and drain salted black beans. Add garlic to black beans. Mash with the handle of a cleaver.

5. Mix ingredients for thickening sauce in a small bowl.

To Cook:

1. In a small saucepan, bring 2 cups water to a boil over high heat. Add ½ teaspoon salt, ½ tablespoon oil, and snow peas. Cook for 30 seconds, drain, and set aside.

2. Heat 3 tablespoons oil in a wok over high heat. Add ginger root, black beans, garlic, and fish. Stir occasionally and gently for 3 minutes or until the fish turns white. Discard the ginger root.

3. Add sauce, snow peas, and green onions. Stir carefully until thickened and serve.

Sweet and Sour Whole Fish (Serves 2 to 3)　糖醋全魚

1 (1½-pound) fresh trout
  or bass, red snapper, flounder
2 teaspoons lemon juice
4 slices peeled ginger root
1 teaspoon salt
1 fresh hot pepper*
1 tomato

Sweet and sour sauce:
  ⅛ teaspoon freshly ground pepper
  ¼ teaspoon salt
  1 tablespoon cornstarch
  3 tablespoons sugar
  ¼ cup cider vinegar
  2 tablespoons soy sauce
  2 tablespoons catsup
  ¾ cup chicken broth
  1 teaspoon sesame oil

¼ cup cornstarch
4 cups oil for deep-frying
2 tablespoons oil
1 tablespoon shredded ginger root
2 cloves garlic, sliced
3 green onions, shredded

To Prepare Ahead:

1. Scale and clean fish; rinse under cold water and blot dry with paper towels. Score fish by making cuts ¼ inch deep at 2-inch intervals on both sides. (Cut fish in half, if too long to fit in wok.)

2. Put lemon juice and ginger root slices in a small bowl. With the back of a spoon, press ginger root hard against the bowl to release the flavorful juice. Rub ginger-lemon juice on fish, inside and out.

3. Sprinkle 1 teaspoon salt over fish, inside and out. Refrigerate for 30 minutes or longer.

4. Cut hot pepper in half lengthwise, remove seeds, and cut into thin shreds. Cut tomato into ¾-inch cubes.

5. Mix ingredients for sweet and sour sauce in a bowl.

6. Coat fish with ¼ cup cornstarch just before deep-frying.

---

* Add more hot peppers, if you like it spicier.

To Cook:

1. Heat 4 cups oil to 375°F. in the wok over high heat. Deep-fry fish until brown, about 12 to 15 minutes. Transfer to an oval platter. (If you cut the fish in half, put the halves back together like a whole fish.)

2. Remove hot oil to a heat-proof bowl. Wipe wok clean with paper towels.

3. Heat 2 tablespoons oil over high heat. Add ginger root shreds, garlic, hot pepper, and tomato. Stir-fry for 1 minute.

4. Pour in sauce. Bring to a boil over high heat, stirring occasionally. Add green onion shreds. Pour sauce mixture over the fish and serve.

Catsup Shrimp (Serves 2 to 3)　茄汁明蝦

　　1 pound large shrimp in shells
　　1 teaspoon salt
　　Dash white pepper

　　Seasoning sauce:
　　　½ teaspoon sugar
　　　1 tablespoon soy sauce
　　　1 tablespoon dry sherry
　　　2 tablespoons catsup

　　3 tablespoons oil
　　2 slices peeled ginger root
　　2 cloves garlic, smashed and peeled
　　3 green onions, cut into 1½-inch pieces

To Prepare Ahead:

1. With a pair of scissors, cut open the back of each shrimp and remove the vein, leaving the shell on. Rinse with cold water. Drain well in a colander.

2. Sprinkle salt and white pepper over shrimp. Mix and refrigerate for 30 minutes or longer.

3. Mix ingredients for seasoning sauce in a small bowl.

To Cook:

1. Heat 3 tablespoons oil in a wok over high heat. Add ginger root and garlic. Then add shrimp, spreading it out in the wok. Stir only occasionally for 3 to 5 minutes or until done. Discard ginger root and garlic.

2. Add sauce and green onions. Stir a few seconds and serve.

Tip　• This dish can also be served cold or at room temperature.

Shrimp Balls with Bean Threads (Serves 4) 粉絲蝦球

Ingredients for shrimp balls:
    1 pound small shrimp in shells
    2 teaspoons chopped ginger root
    3 ounces ground pork
    ⅛ teaspoon freshly ground pepper
    1 teaspoon salt
    2 tablespoons cornstarch
    1 teaspoon dry sherry
    ½ teaspoon lemon juice
    1 egg white
    3 cups oil for deep-frying

2 ounces bean threads
1 pound Chinese cabbage
2 tablespoons oil
1 teaspoon salt
1½ cups chicken broth

To Prepare Ahead:

1. Follow the recipe for **Deep-Fried Shrimp Balls** (page 47). This can be done in advance.

2. Soak bean threads in 4 cups hot water for 10 minutes; drain and discard water.

3. Rinse, drain, and cut Chinese cabbage crosswise into 1-inch pieces.

To Cook:

1. Heat 2 tablespoons oil in a wok over high heat. Add cabbage and 1 teaspoon salt, and stir-fry for 1 minute.

2. Add bean threads, shrimp balls, and broth to the wok; stir twice. Bring to a boil, turn heat to medium, cover, and cook for 5 minutes.

3. Transfer cabbage and bean threads to a serving dish. Top with shrimp balls.

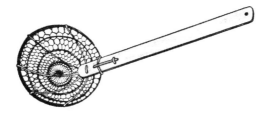

Shrimp over Sizzling Rice (Serves 4)　　蝦仁鍋巴

    3 cups boiled rice (page 155)
    1 pound medium shrimp in shells
    1 teaspoon salt
    1 carrot
    10 water chestnuts

Sauce:

    2 tablespoons cornstarch
    ⅛ teaspoon freshly ground pepper
    ½ teaspoon sesame oil
    1 teaspoon dry sherry
    1 tablespoon soy sauce
    ¼ cup catsup
    ½ cup water
    1½ cups chicken broth

    4 tablespoons oil
    ½ cup green peas, fresh or frozen
    ½ cup canned sliced mushrooms
    4 slices peeled ginger root
    1 green onion, chopped
    3 cups oil for deep-frying

To Bake Rice Patties:

1. Spread freshly boiled rice in a heavy roasting pan (11 x 14 inches) and press it hard with a spatula. (Dip the spatula into water as needed to prevent it from sticking to the rice.)

2. Bake uncovered at 400°F. oven for 35 to 60 minutes or until rice has formed a solid, hard crust and edges have loosened from the roasting pan.

3. When cool, break into smaller pieces.

To Prepare Ahead:

1. Shell, devein, rinse, and drain shrimp. Sprinkle with ½ teaspoon salt and mix well. Refrigerate for 30 minutes or longer.

2. Peel carrot, quarter lengthwise, and cut diagonally into ½-inch pieces. Quarter water chestnuts.

3. Mix sauce ingredients in a bowl.

To Cook:

1. Heat 1 tablespoon oil in a wok over high heat. Add carrot, water chestnuts, peas, mushrooms, and ½ teaspoon salt. Stir-fry for 3 minutes. Transfer to a plate.

2. Clean and dry the wok; heat 3 tablespoons oil over high heat. Add ginger

root, green onion, and shrimp. Stir-fry for 3 minutes or until the shrimp turn pink. Discard the ginger root. Transfer shrimp to the plate with vegetables.

3. Bring sauce to a boil in the wok, stirring occasionally. Return shrimp and vegetables to the wok. Serve with deep-fried rice patties.

To Deep-Fry Rice Patties:

Heat 3 cups oil to 375°F. in a wok over high heat. Deep-fry rice patties a few seconds until they whiten and puff up. Drain and transfer to a large deep dish.

To Serve:

At the dinner table, pour the shrimp over deep-fried rice patties immediately. The rice will sizzle if it is very hot.

Tip • You can bake rice patties in advance. They will keep in a covered container for a week.

Stir-Fried Shrimp with Onion (Serves 2 to 3)　洋葱蝦仁

    1 pound medium shrimp in shells
    1 teaspoon salt
    1 onion

    Thickening sauce:
      1 teaspoon cornstarch
      4 tablespoons water

    4 tablespoons oil
    2 slices peeled ginger root

To Prepare Ahead:

1. Shell, devein, rinse, and drain shrimp. Add ¾ teaspoon salt and mix well. Refrigerate for 30 minutes or longer.

2. Cut onion lengthwise into 12 sections and separate into layers.

3. Mix ingredients for thickening sauce in a small bowl.

To Cook:

1. Heat 1 tablespoon oil in a wok over high heat. Add onion and ¼ teaspoon salt, and stir for 2 minutes. Transfer to a plate.

2. Wipe the wok with a paper towel. Add 3 tablespoons oil. When hot, add ginger root; after 20 seconds, add shrimp. Stir-fry 2 to 3 minutes or until shrimp turn pink. Discard the ginger root.

3. Return onion to the wok and pour in sauce. Stir until thickened and serve.

Shrimp with Cashews (Serves 2 to 3)　　腰果蝦仁

    1 pound medium shrimp in shells
    ½ teaspoon salt
    1 teaspoon lemon juice
    15 water chestnuts

Thickening sauce:
    Dash white pepper
    1 teaspoon cornstarch
    ¼ teaspoon salt
    1 teaspoon dry sherry
    ½ teaspoon sesame oil
    3 tablespoons chicken broth

    3 tablespoons oil
    4 slices peeled ginger root
    2 green onions, cut into 1-inch pieces
    ½ cup roasted cashews

To Prepare Ahead:

1. Shell, devein, rinse, and drain shrimp. Sprinkle with ½ teaspoon salt and lemon juice; mix well. Refrigerate for 30 minutes.

2. Quarter water chestnuts.

3. Mix sauce ingredients in a small bowl.

To Cook:

1. Heat 3 tablespoons oil in a wok over high heat. Add ginger root, green onions, and shrimp. Stir-fry for 2 minutes. Add water chestnuts and stir-fry for 1 minute. Discard the ginger root.

2. Add sauce, stir until thickened and transfer to a plate. Spread cashews on top and serve.

Shrimp with Lobster Sauce* (Serves 2 to 3)　豉 汁 蝦 仁

1 pound medium shrimp in shells
¾ teaspoon salt
2 teaspoons salted black beans
2 cloves garlic, smashed and peeled

Sauce:

2 teaspoons cornstarch
¼ teaspoon sugar
½ teaspoon lemon juice
2 teaspoons dry sherry
2 teaspoons soy sauce
½ cup chicken broth
Dash freshly ground pepper

3 tablespoons oil
3 ounces lean ground pork
1 egg
1 green onion, finely chopped

To Prepare Ahead:

1. Shell, devein, rinse, and drain shrimp. Sprinkle with salt and mix well.

2. Rinse and drain salted black beans. Combine beans with garlic in a rice bowl and mash with the handle of a cleaver.

3. Mix sauce ingredients in a small bowl.

To Cook:

1. Heat 3 tablespoons oil in a wok over high heat. Add black beans and garlic; then add shrimp and pork. Stir-fry for 2 to 3 minutes or until shrimp turn pink.

2. Pour in sauce and stir until it bubbles.

3. Add egg, stir slowly for a few seconds. Transfer to a serving dish. Sprinkle with chopped green onion and serve with rice.

---

* The name is somewhat confusing. Actually the sauce contains no lobster, but is the same sauce used for **Lobster Cantonese** (page 140).

Stir-Fried Shrimp with Mushrooms (Serves 2)   蘑菇蝦仁

½ pound medium shrimp in shells
1 teaspoon salt
Dash white pepper
1 teaspoon lemon juice
8 ounces fresh mushrooms
1 cucumber

Thickening sauce:
  2 teaspoons cornstarch
  3 tablespoons water
  1 teaspoon soy sauce

5 tablespoons oil
1 clove garlic, sliced
2 slices peeled ginger root
1 green onion, cut into 1-inch pieces

To Prepare Ahead:

1. Shell, devein, rinse, and drain shrimp. Sprinkle with ¼ teaspoon salt, white pepper, and lemon juice; mix well. Refrigerate for 30 minutes or longer.

2. Slice mushrooms into ½-inch pieces.

3. Peel cucumber and cut in half lengthwise. Remove seeds and cut diagonally into ¼-inch-thick slices.

4. Mix ingredients for thickening sauce in a small bowl.

To Cook:

1. Heat 1 tablespoon oil in a wok over high heat. Add garlic, cucumber, and ¼ teaspoon salt. Stir-fry for 1 minute. Transfer to a plate.

2. Wipe the wok with a paper towel. Add 2 tablespoons oil. When hot, add mushrooms and ½ teaspoon salt, and stir-fry for 1 minute. Set aside with cucumber.

3. Rinse and dry the wok; pour in 2 tablespoons oil. When hot, add ginger root, green onion, and shrimp. Stir-fry until shrimp turn pink, about 2 minutes. Discard the ginger root.

4. Return vegetables to the wok and pour in sauce. Stir until thickened and serve.

Stir-Fried Shrimp with Eggs (Serves 2 to 3)　蝦仁炒蛋

　　1 pound medium shrimp in shells
　　¾ teaspoon salt
　　Dash white pepper

Egg mixture:
　　¼ teaspoon salt
　　4 eggs
　　2 green onions, chopped
　　2 tablespoons water

　　5 tablespoons oil
　　2 slices peeled ginger root

To Prepare Ahead:

1. Shell, devein, rinse, and drain shrimp. Sprinkle with ¾ teaspoon salt and pepper; mix well. Refrigerate for 30 minutes or longer.

2. In a mixing bowl, combine egg mixture and hand beat for 1 minute.

To Cook:

1. Heat 2 tablespoons oil in a wok over high heat. Pour in egg mixture, stirring for about 1 minute or less. (It should be very soft and a little creamy.) Remove from wok.

2. Heat 3 tablespoons oil over high heat. Add ginger root; after 20 seconds, add shrimp. Stir-fry for about 3 minutes or until shrimp turn pink. Discard the ginger root.

3. Return eggs to the wok, mix well, and serve.

Rice

Boiled Rice (Serves 3 to 4)　白　飯

> 1 cup enriched, long grain white rice
> 1¾ cups water (Use 1½ cups water, if boiling rice to make fried rice.)

1. Measure rice into a 2- to 3-quart saucepan. Rinse with cold water a couple of times.

2. Drain well and add 1¾ cups water. Cover and bring to a boil over high heat.

3. Reduce heat to medium-low, cover halfway, and cook for 5 minutes or until water is almost absorbed.

4. Cover tightly, reduce heat to low, and cook for 10 minutes more. (Do not lift lid.)

5. Turn heat off and let stand for 10 minutes without lifting the lid. It is important to let the steam continue cooking the rice.

Tips
- 1 cup raw rice yields 3 cups boiled rice.

- When you increase the amount of rice, add only 1½ cups water for each additional cup of rice. (For example, to cook 2 cups rice, use 3¼ cups water.)

Basic Fried Rice (Serves 4)　蛋　炒　飯

> 2 eggs
> 3 tablespoons oil
> 2 green onions, chopped
> 3 cups boiled rice (see recipe above), room temperature
> ½ teaspoon salt
> 1 tablespoon soy sauce

1. Beat eggs lightly.

2. Heat 3 tablespoons oil in a wok over high heat. Add green onions and eggs, and stir for 10 to 20 seconds.

3. Add rice and stir briskly for 2 minutes more. Season with salt and soy sauce, mix well and serve.

Tips
- Substitute 1 tablespoon brown sauce or 1 tablespoon dark soy sauce for 1 tablespoon soy sauce, if you like a darker color.

- Fried rice can be prepared in advance and reheated.

Barbecued Pork Fried Rice (Serves 4 to 6)　叉燒炒飯

      1 cup diced barbecued pork (page 98)
      2 eggs
      3 tablespoons oil
      2 green onions, chopped
      3 cups boiled rice (page 155), room temperature
      ½ teaspoon salt
      1 tablespoon soy sauce

1. Beat eggs lightly.

2. Heat 3 tablespoons oil in a wok over high heat. Add green onions and eggs, and stir for 10 to 20 seconds.

3. Add rice and diced pork; stir briskly for 2 minutes. Season with salt and soy sauce; mix well and serve.

Beef Fried Rice (Serves 4 to 6)　牛肉炒飯

      2 eggs
      ½ cup frozen peas and carrots
      1 teaspoon salt
      3 tablespoons oil
      ½ pound lean ground beef
      2 green onions, chopped
      3 cups boiled rice (page 155), room temperature
      1 tablespoon soy sauce

1. Beat eggs lightly.

2. In a small saucepan, bring 1 cup water to a boil. Add peas, carrots, and ¼ teaspoon salt. Cook over medium heat for 1 minute and drain.

3. Heat 1 tablespoon oil in a wok over high heat. Add ground beef and ¼ teaspoon salt, and brown. Drain off excess fat and transfer beef to a bowl.

4. Rinse and dry the wok; heat 2 tablespoons oil over high heat. Add green onions and eggs, and stir for 10 to 20 seconds.

5. Add rice and stir briskly for 1 to 2 minutes or until rice is heated through.

6. Return beef, peas, and carrots to the wok. Add ½ teaspoon salt and soy sauce. Mix well and serve.

Chicken Fried Rice (Serves 4 to 6)　鶏丁炒飯

½ chicken breast, boned and skinned*

Marinade for chicken:
    1 teaspoon cornstarch
    1 teaspoon soy sauce
    1 teaspoon dry sherry
    2 teaspoons water

¼ pound fresh mung bean sprouts
2 eggs
4 tablespoons oil
2 green onions, chopped
3 cups boiled rice (page 155), room temperature
¾ teaspoon salt
1 tablespoon soy sauce

To Prepare Ahead:

1. Dice chicken into ¼-inch pieces.

2. Transfer the chicken to a mixing bowl. Add marinade ingredients and toss to coat thoroughly. Let stand for 5 minutes or longer.

3. Snap off the root ends of bean sprouts. Rinse bean sprouts in a pot of cold water and drain. Pile trimmed bean sprouts on a chopping board; cut at ½-inch intervals.

4. Beat eggs lightly.

To Cook:

1. Heat 1 tablespoon oil in a wok over high heat. Add bean sprouts and stir-fry for 1 minute or less. Transfer to a colander to drain.

2. Wipe the wok with a paper towel; heat 1 tablespoon oil over high heat. Add chicken. Stir-fry until chicken turns white and firm. Transfer chicken to a plate.

3. Rinse and dry the wok; heat 2 tablespoons oil over high heat. Add green onions and eggs, and stir for 10 to 20 seconds.

4. Add rice and stir briskly for 2 minutes or until rice is heated.

5. Return chicken and bean sprouts to the wok. Add salt and 1 tablespoon soy sauce. Mix well and serve.

* See directions on page 115.

Ham and Shrimp Fried Rice (Serves 4 to 6)　火腿蝦仁炒飯

>   4 ounces cooked ham
>   ½ pound small shrimp in shells
>   2 eggs
>   ½ cup green peas, fresh or frozen
>   1 teaspoon salt
>   5 tablespoons oil
>   2 green onions, chopped
>   3 cups boiled rice (page 155), room temperature
>   1 tablespoon soy sauce

To Prepare Ahead:

1. Dice ham into ¼-inch pieces.

2. Shell, devein, and rinse shrimp. Cut into pieces the size of peas.

3. Beat eggs lightly.

To Cook:

1. In small saucepan, bring 1 cup water to a boil. Add peas and ¼ teaspoon salt. Cook over medium heat for 1 minute and drain.

2. Heat 2 tablespoons oil in a wok over high heat. Add shrimp and ¼ teaspoon salt, and stir-fry until shrimp turn pink. Transfer to a plate.

3. Rinse and dry the wok; heat 3 tablespoons oil over high heat . Add green onions and eggs, and stir for 10 to 20 seconds.

4. Add rice and ham, and stir briskly for 2 minutes or until rice is heated through.

5. Return shrimp to wok. Add peas, ½ teaspoon salt, and soy sauce. Mix well and serve.

Tip • If you omit ham, you will have **Shrimp Fried Rice.**

Noodles and Dough

Assorted Chow Mein (Serves 4)　什錦炒麵

> ½ pound medium shrimp in shells
> 1 teaspoon salt
> 6 Chinese dried mushrooms
> 5 ounces Chinese noodles
>
> *Seasonings for noodles:*
> > ¼ teaspoon salt
> > 1 tablespoon soy sauce
> > 1 teaspoon sesame oil
>
> 4 ounces barbecued pork (page 98)
> 4 ounces fresh snow peas
> 4 ounces bok choy
>
> *Sauce:*
> > 1 tablespoon cornstarch
> > 1 tablespoon soy sauce
> > 1 cup chicken broth
>
> 5 tablespoons oil
> 1 slice peeled ginger root
> 1 clove garlic, smashed and peeled
> 2 green onions, cut into 1½-inch pieces

To Prepare Ahead:

1. Shell, devein, rinse, and drain shrimp. Sprinkle with ½ teaspoon salt; mix thoroughly. Refrigerate for 30 minutes or longer.

2. Soak dried mushrooms in a bowl of hot water for 20 minutes. Rinse and squeeze dry. Cut off the stems. Shred the caps into thin strips and add to the shrimp mixture.

3. In a 3-quart saucepan, bring 1 quart of water to a boil over high heat. Add noodles and disperse with a pair of chopsticks or a fork. Cook uncovered for 3 to 5 minutes. Drain and rinse with cold running water, and drain again. Transfer to a mixing bowl. Add the noodle seasonings and mix thoroughly.

4. Cut barbecued pork into ¾ x 2-inch slices, ⅛ inch thick.

5. Remove tips and strings from the snow peas. Cut bok choy diagonally into pieces 2 inches long and ¼ inch thick.

6. Mix sauce ingredients in a bowl.

To Cook:

1. Heat 2 tablespoons oil in a wok over high heat. Add noodles, and stir occasionally for 3 minutes. Transfer to a platter and keep warm in the oven.

160

2. Rinse and dry the wok. Add 1 tablespoon oil. When hot, add bok choy, snow peas, and ½ teaspoon salt. Stir-fry for 2 minutes and transfer to a plate.

3. Wipe the wok with a paper towel. Heat 2 tablespoons oil. Add ginger root and garlic; after a few seconds, add shrimp and mushrooms. Stir-fry until shrimp turn pink. Discard the ginger root and garlic.

4. Add to the wok: barbecued pork, green onions, vegetables, and sauce, stirring occasionally until thickened. Pour the mixture over noodles and serve.

Beef Pan-Fried Noodles (Serves 4)　滑牛兩面黃

½ pound flank steak
Marinade for beef:
　　2 teaspoons cornstarch
　　2 teaspoons water
　　2 teaspoons dry sherry
　　1 tablespoon soy sauce
　　1 tablespoon oil
5 ounces thin Chinese noodles
Seasonings for noodles:
　　¼ teaspoon salt
　　1 tablespoon soy sauce
　　1 teaspoon sesame oil

½ pound fresh asparagus (or celery)
15 water chestnuts
Sauce:
　　1 tablespoon cornstarch
　　2 tablespoons oyster sauce
　　1 cup chicken broth

6 tablespoons oil
½ teaspoon salt
1 slice peeled ginger root
4 green onions, cut into 1½-inch pieces

To Prepare Ahead:

1. Cut flank steak lengthwise into strips 1½ inches wide; then cut across the grain into ⅛-inch slices.

2. Transfer steak to a mixing bowl. Add marinade ingredients and toss to coat thoroughly. Let stand for 30 minutes or longer.

3. In a 3-quart saucepan, bring 1 quart of water to a boil over high heat. Add

noodles and disperse with a pair of chopsticks or a fork. Cook uncovered for 3 to 4 minutes. Drain, rinse with cold running water, and drain again. Transfer to a mixing bowl. Add the noodle seasonings and mix thoroughly.

4. Snap off tough ends of the asparagus. Rinse and roll-cut into 1½-inch pieces. (If using celery, slice diagonally ¼ inch thick.)

5. Slice water chestnuts.

6. Mix sauce ingredients in a bowl.

To Cook:

1. In a large non-stick skillet, heat 2 tablespoons oil over high heat. Add noodles, turn heat to medium, and brown undisturbed for 4 minutes.

2. Flip noodles over. Add 1 tablespoon oil and swirl to spread oil evenly. Brown for 4 minutes. Transfer to a platter.

3. Heat 1 tablespoon oil in a wok over high heat. Add asparagus, water chestnuts, and ½ teaspoon salt, and stir constantly for 1 to 2 minutes. Transfer to a plate.

4. Wipe the wok clean with a paper towel. Heat 2 tablespoons oil over high heat. Add ginger root, green onions; after a few seconds, add beef. Stir-fry for 1 minute. Discard the ginger root and set beef aside with the vegetables.

5. Add sauce to the wok, and stir until it bubbles. Return the vegetables and beef to the wok and immediately pour the mixture over the noodles and serve.

Chicken Chow Mein (Serves 4) 鷄 絲 炒 麵

½ pound chicken breast, boned and skinned*

Marinade for chicken:
>   2 teaspoons cornstarch
>   1 teaspoon soy sauce
>   1 teaspoon dry sherry
>   2 teaspoons water

5 ounces Chinese noodles

Seasonings for noodles:
>   ¼ teaspoon salt
>   1 tablespoon soy sauce
>   1 teaspoon sesame oil

2 stalks celery
¼ pound fresh mung bean sprouts

See directions on page 115. You need almost 1 pound of chicken breast with bone and skin to get ½ pound of meat.

Sauce:

    1 tablespoon cornstarch
    1 tablespoon soy sauce
    1 cup chicken broth

6 tablespoons oil
½ teaspoon salt
1 clove garlic, smashed and peeled
3 green onions, cut into 1½-inch pieces

To Prepare Ahead:

1. Slice chicken by cutting across the grain into pieces ⅛ inch thick and 2 inches long. Then cut into strips, ⅛ x ⅛ x 2 inches.

2. Transfer chicken to a mixing bowl. Add marinade ingredients and toss to coat thoroughly. Let stand for 30 minutes or longer.

3. In a 3-quart saucepan, bring 1 quart of water to a boil over high heat. Add noodles and disperse with a pair of chopsticks or a fork. Cook uncovered for 3 to 5 minutes. Drain, rinse with cold running water, and drain again. Transfer to a mixing bowl. Add the noodle seasonings and mix thoroughly.

4. Rinse and shred celery. Rinse bean sprouts in a pot of cold water and drain well.

5. Mix sauce ingredients in a bowl.

To Cook:

1. Heat 2 tablespoons oil in a wok over high heat. Add noodles and stir occasionally for 3 minutes. Transfer to a platter and keep warm in the oven.

2. Rinse and dry the wok. Add 2 tablespoons oil. When hot, add bean sprouts, celery, and ½ teaspoon salt. Stir-fry for 2 minutes and transfer to a plate.

3. Wipe the wok with a paper towel. Add 2 tablespoons oil. When hot, add garlic and green onions; after a few seconds, add chicken shreds. Stir-fry for 2 to 3 minutes or until chicken turns white and firm. Discard the garlic.

4. Add sauce, stirring until thickened. Return vegetables to the wok. Pour the mixture over noodles and serve.

Boiled Dumplings (Yields 30, serves 2 to 3) 水 餃

Dough:
 2 cups all-purpose flour
 ¾ cup water

½ pound Chinese cabbage
¾ pound lean ground pork

Seasoning ingredients:
 1 teaspoon salt
 2 teaspoons cornstarch
 ¼ teaspoon minced ginger root
 1 teaspoon dry sherry
 2 tablespoons finely chopped green onions
 2 tablespoons soy sauce
 1 tablespoon sesame oil
 Dash freshly ground pepper

Dipping sauce:
 2 tablespoons soy sauce
 2 tablespoons white vinegar
 1 teaspoon sesame oil
 2 teaspoons hot bean sauce (optional)

To Make Dough:

In a large mixing bowl, combine flour and water; and mix until a dough forms. Knead for a couple of minutes on a floured surface. Cover with a damp cloth and let stand for 30 minutes.

To Make Filling:

In a saucepan, bring 2 cups water to a boil over high heat. Add Chinese cabbage, cook for 2 minutes and drain. When cool, squeeze out water. Chop cabbage finely. In a mixing bowl, thoroughly mix pork, chopped cabbage, and seasoning ingredients.

To Assemble:

1. Place dough on a floured surface and knead for 5 minutes.

2. Divide dough into 2 portions. Shape each into a cylinder about 1 foot long.

3. Cut each roll of dough into about fifteen ¾-inch pieces.

4. Roll each piece into a ball; then flatten slightly.

5. With a rolling pin, roll each piece into a 3-inch circle.

6. Assemble as shown in the pictures. (a) Put 1 tablespoon filling in the center. (b) Pinch points A and A' together. (c) Pinch B and B' together and C and C' together. (d) Pleat edge A'-B' and seal to edge A-B; pleat edge A'-C' and seal to edge A-C. (e) Press the edges together firmly.

(a)

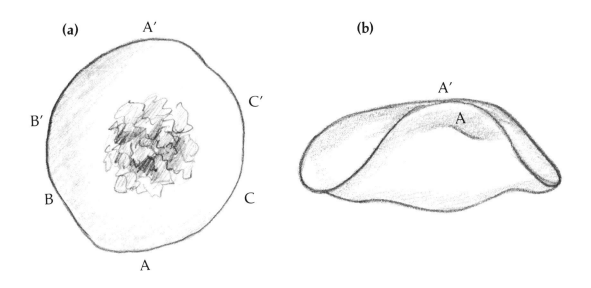

(b)

(c)

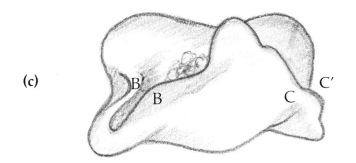

(d)

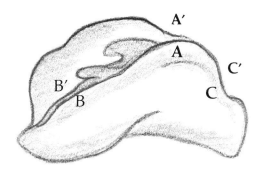

(e)

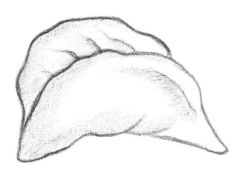

7. Lightly flour a cookie sheet and place dumplings on the sheet not touching each other.

To Cook:

1. In a Dutch oven or 6-quart pot, bring 3 quarts water to a boil over high heat.

2. Add dumplings one by one. Stir once carefully with a wooden spoon to make sure they do not stick to the bottom of the pot.

3. Cover and bring to a boil. Before it boils over, pour in 1 cup tap water.

4. Repeat step 3 two more times. Total cooking time is about 10 minutes. To test doneness, remove a dumpling and cut apart. If the pork is no longer pink, the dumplings are done.

5. With a slotted spoon, remove boiled dumplings to two platters.

6. Make dipping sauce. Serve dumplings hot with dipping sauce. The water in which the dumplings are cooked can be served at the end of the meal to quench your thirst after eating the salty dip.

Tips
- Assembled dumplings can be refrigerated for a day or frozen for weeks. To store, place on a floured surface without touching each other. Thaw completely before cooking.

- Leftover boiled dumplings can be reheated by pan-frying in a non-stick skillet with 1 to 2 tablespoons oil; cover and cook over medium heat for 3 to 4 minutes or until the bottoms are golden brown. They will taste very much like the **Pan-Fried Dumplings** (see next page).

- The individual place setting for this meal should include a pair of chopsticks, a soup spoon on a saucer, and a rice bowl.

- Boiled dumplings, a typical Northern Chinese dish, is a complete meal by itself.

Pan-Fried Dumplings (Yields 30)   鍋 貼

Dough:
   2 cups all-purpose flour
   ¾ cup water

½ pound Chinese cabbage
¾ pound lean ground pork

Seasoning ingredients:
   1 teaspoon salt
   2 teaspoons cornstarch
   ¼ teaspoon minced ginger root
   1 teaspoon dry sherry
   2 tablespoons finely chopped green onions
   2 tablespoons soy sauce
   1 tablespoon sesame oil
   Dash freshly ground pepper

4 tablespoons oil
1½ cups chicken broth

Dipping sauce:
   2 tablespoons soy sauce
   2 tablespoons white vinegar
   1 teaspoon sesame oil
   2 teaspoons hot bean sauce (optional)

To Make Dough, Filling, and Assemble:

See recipe for **Boiled Dumplings** (pages 164 and 165).

To Cook:

1. Heat 2 tablespoons oil in a large non-stick skillet over medium heat. Arrange 15 dumplings, pleated side up, in the skillet. Cook uncovered for 1 to 2 minutes or until browned on the bottom.

2. Add ¾ cup chicken broth, cover tightly, and cook for 4 minutes.

3. Remove lid and cook until all the liquid is absorbed.

4. Transfer dumplings, brown side up, to a plate. Cover with aluminum foil to keep warm.

5. Pan-fry the rest of dumplings the same way.

6. Make dipping sauce. Serve dumplings hot with dipping sauce.

Tips • You can substitute ¾ pound lean ground beef for pork.

   • Dumplings can be frozen after pan-frying. Reheat in 350°F. oven for 15 minutes or in a microwave oven.

Mandarin Pancakes (Yields 20)   薄 餅

    3 cups sifted all-purpose flour
    1¼ cups boiling water
    1 tablespoon sesame oil

1. In a large mixing bowl, combine flour and boiling water; mix with a wooden spoon. When it cools a little, knead into a soft dough. Transfer to a lightly floured surface and knead gently for 3 minutes, adding more flour when needed.

2. Cover dough with a damp cloth and let stand for 15 minutes.

3. Knead again for 2 minutes. With a rolling pin, roll dough ¼ inch thick. Cut the dough into 20 circles using a 2½-inch diameter cookie cutter or a coffee cup.

4. Brush half the circles with sesame oil and place the unoiled ones on top.

5. Using a rolling pin, flatten each pair into a circle about 6 inches in diameter.

6. Place a heavy skillet over medium heat. Cook pancakes one at a time in the ungreased skillet, turning it over after about 1 minute or when it puffs up and little brown spots appear on the bottom. Cook another minute.

7. Transfer pancakes to a plate, and cover with aluminum foil to keep moist and warm.

8. Separate the two layers carefully when serving.

Tips • Cooking pancakes in pairs makes the inside moist and assures a paper-thin pancake.

  • You can freeze pancakes after they are cooked. Separate the two layers carefully and fold into quarters. Store in an airtight plastic bag or container. Thaw and reheat in foil for about 15 minutes in a 425°F. oven.

Steamed Flower Rolls (Yields 16)   花 捲

    1 tablespoon sugar
    ⅓ cup lukewarm water
    1 package dry yeast
    4 cups all-purpose flour
    1 cup lukewarm milk
    1 tablespoon oil
    ½ teaspoon salt

To Make Dough:

1. Dissolve sugar in lukewarm water. Sprinkle with yeast and let stand for 5 minutes.

168

2. In a large mixing bowl, combine flour, lukewarm milk, and yeast mixture. Mix until a dough forms.

3. Transfer dough to a floured surface and knead for 4 minutes.

4. Return dough to the mixing bowl and cover with a damp cloth. Set aside in a warm place and let rise until it doubles in volume, about 2 hours.

5. Punch the dough down with your fist to reduce it back to its original volume. Cover and let rest for 20 minutes.

6. Transfer dough to floured surface and knead for 2 minutes.

To Make Flower Rolls:

1. Divide dough into 2 portions.

2. With a rolling pin, roll dough into a 10 x 12-inch rectangle.

3. Brush ½ tablespoon oil over the surface; then sprinkle with ¼ teaspoon salt.

4. Roll dough up lengthwise, like a jellyroll. Cut into 8 rounds, 1½ inches long.

5. Lay a chopstick on top of the round parallel to the cut edges. Press the chopstick down firmly. The oiled layers will separate like petals.

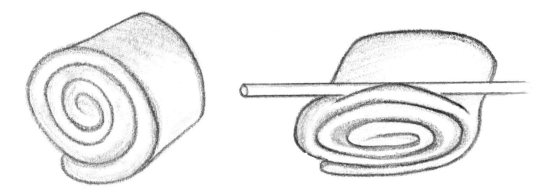

6. Repeat steps 2 to 5 with other half of dough.

To Steam:

1. Bring 2 quarts water to a boil in a steamer over high heat.

2. Arrange 8 flower rolls about 1 inch apart on each tier of the steamer. Cover and steam for 8 minutes. Serve with **Szechwan Crisp Duck** (page 136) or eat as you would bread.

Tip • After steaming, the flower rolls can be frozen. To reheat, repeat the steaming procedure. However, the frozen rolls can be placed close together on one tier without defrosting.

Desserts

Almond Cookies (Yields 3 dozen) 杏 仁 餅

1¼ cups Crisco shortening, at room temperature
1 cup granulated sugar
1½ teaspoons almond extract
1 egg

Dry ingredients:
2 cups all-purpose flour
1 teaspoon baking powder
½ teaspoon baking soda
¼ teaspoon salt

36 whole blanched almonds

Egg mixture:
1 whole egg
1 egg yolk

1. Preheat oven to 350°F. In a large mixing bowl, cream Crisco shortening and sugar thoroughly with a large spoon.

2. Add almond extract and 1 whole egg, mixing well.

3. Combine dry ingredients and add to creamed mixture. Mix with your fingers until a dough forms.

4. Roll dough into 1-inch balls. Place on an ungreased cookie sheet about 2 inches apart.

5. Place an almond in the center of each ball, pressing down gently but firmly. Brush each ball with beaten egg mixture.

6. Bake at 350°F. for 12 to 15 minutes. Cool for 10 minutes and remove from cookie sheet with a spatula.

Tip • Almond cookies will keep for a week in an airtight container or for months in the freezer.

Almond Float (Serves 4) 杏 仁 豆 腐

1 envelope unflavored gelatin (1 tablespoon)
¼ cup sugar
1 cup boiling water
1 cup milk
¼ to ½ teaspoon almond extract
1 cup fruit cocktail with syrup
   or other fruit

1. In a mixing bowl, combine gelatin and sugar.

2. Add boiling water and stir until gelatin and sugar dissolve.

3. Add milk and almond extract, and mix thoroughly.

4. Transfer to a flat container and chill until firm.

5. Cut into ½ x ½-inch squares. Use a spatula to loosen squares.

6. Divide the almond float among four dessert bowls. Top with canned fruit cocktail or fresh fruit (see below).

Tips   • Instead of fruit cocktail, use Mandarin orange sections, peach slices, pineapple chunks or other canned fruit. You can also use fresh fruit, such as strawberries, banana slices, watermelon chunks, cantaloupe chunks, etc. When using fresh fruit, make a syrup of ½ cup ice water and 2 tablespoons sugar; mix with fruit, and spoon over almond float.

      • This dessert can be made 2 to 3 days in advance (through step 4).

Eight-Treasure Rice Pudding   (Serves 10 to 12)   八 寶 飯

    2 cups sweet rice
    3 cups water
    ¼ cup sugar
    4 tablespoons Crisco shortening
    1 (9-ounce) can sweetened red bean paste

Treasures:
    8 dried red dates
    3 preserved black dates, pitted
    4 pieces preserved longan pulp
    1 tablespoon candied citrus fruit peel
    20 raisins
    1 candied cherry

Syrup:
    1 tablespoon cornstarch
    1 cup water
    ¼ cup sugar
    ¼ teaspoon almond extract

To Prepare Ahead:

1. Put rice in a 3-quart saucepan, rinse with cold water, and drain well. Add 3 cups water, cover, and bring to a boil over high heat.

2. Reduce heat to medium, half-cover, and cook for 5 to 8 minutes or until the water is almost absorbed.

3. Turn heat to low, cover tightly, and cook for 10 minutes.

4. Turn heat off and let stand covered for 10 minutes more.

5. Add ¼ cup sugar and 2 tablespoons Crisco shortening to the rice; mix thoroughly.

6. In a wok or skillet, mix sweetened red bean paste and 2 tablespoons Crisco shortening over medium heat for 2 minutes.

7. In a small saucepan, cook dried red dates in ½ cup water for 3 minutes. Cut in half and remove pits. Cut black dates in half.

To Mold:

1. Line a 1-quart heat-proof bowl with plastic wrap. Spread two-thirds of sweet rice in the bowl. Add sweetened red bean paste to the center and cover with remaining rice.

2. Place another sheet of plastic wrap on top of the rice; then invert a dinner plate over the bowl. Grasp the edges of both bowl and plate and turn over.

3. Lift bowl and wrap off to unmold the pudding. Decorate top and sides with the "treasures." (See picture on pages 28 and 29.)

4. Gently spread the wrap back over the pudding. Invert the bowl and set it over the pudding. Turn over, remove the plate, and refrigerate until ready to steam.

To Steam:

Bring 1 gallon of water to a boil in a steamer over high heat. Place pudding (still in the heat-proof bowl) on a tier of steamer and steam for 1 hour.

To Make Syrup:

1. Combine cornstarch and 1 cup water in a small saucepan, and stir until completely dissolved.

2. Add ¼ cup sugar. Bring to a boil over medium heat, stirring constantly.

3. Remove from heat and add ¼ teaspoon almond extract.

To Serve:

Unmold pudding onto a plate, pour syrup over it, and serve hot.

Tips • After being molded, pudding can be kept in the refrigerator for several days or frozen for months. Thaw completely and steam.

• This dessert is called **Eight-Treasure Rice Pudding** because we normally use eight different kinds of dried, preserved or candied fruit to make a design on top and sides of the pudding. You can use any of the following: red dates, black dates, lotus seeds, longan pulp, prunes, figs, raisins or candied fruit (citrus peel, melon, pineapple or cherries). You can use less than eight "treasures" and still have authentic rice pudding. The essential ingredients are sweet rice and sweetened red bean paste.

Spun Apples or Spun Bananas (Serves 4)　　拔絲蘋菓或拔絲香蕉

    2 medium-sized golden delicious apples
      or 2 firm bananas

Batter:
    1 egg, beaten
    ¼ cup flour
    ¼ cup cornstarch
    1 teaspoon baking powder
    2 tablespoons water

Sugar mixture:
    ¾ cup sugar
    ¼ cup water
    2 tablespoons oil

    2 cups oil for deep-frying
    3 cups ice water

1. Peel and core apples; cut into 8 wedges. (If using bananas, peel and cut in diagonal slices 1 inch thick.)

2. Combine batter ingredients, and mix until smooth and creamy. Add fruit to the batter.

3. In a small saucepan, combine sugar mixture. Cook over high heat, stirring until sugar dissolves and mixture comes to a boil. Continue cooking, without stirring, until it reaches the hard-crack stage (300°F.). Keep the mixture at 300°F. over the lowest heat.

4. Heat 2 cups oil over high heat to 375°F. in a deep-fryer or wok. Add half of coated fruit pieces, one by one, to the hot oil and deep-fry for 1 to 2 minutes or until lightly brown.

5. Immediately transfer deep-fried fruit pieces into hot syrup. Coat evenly and drop them, one by one, into a bowl of ice water which will harden the syrup coating instantly. Transfer to a lightly greased serving plate.

6. Repeat with rest of fruit pieces. Serve at once.

GARNISHES

Garnishes can transform an ordinary dish into a rich and elegant one. The garnishes must be fresh and presented properly. They can be as simple as sprigs of cilantro, or as elaborate as a carved carrot rose; but all garnishes should be edible. A stir-fried meat and vegetable dish does not need a garnish; garnishes are mainly for dishes containing only meat, poultry, or seafood.

Cilantro can be tucked under the food around the edge of the plate, or several sprigs can be put on top of the food.

Green onions are the most common garnish for Chinese dishes. They can be used in the following ways:

Chopped or shredded green onions are sprinkled over foods such as **Egg Drop Soup** or **Steamed Fish**.

A double brush (b) is made from a 3-inch piece of the white part of the onion. Make three 1-inch cuts on each end (a). Refrigerate in ice water for an hour. Both ends will open up like a pastry brush.

(a)   **(b)**   **(c)**

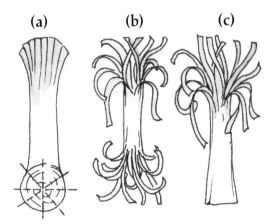

A single brush (c) is made like a double brush but cut only at one end. After it opens up, you can slip a ring of red pepper over the uncut end for a more colorful garnish.

Tomato wedges can be used as a garnish. You can also make a tomato rose. Peel a whole red ripe tomato in a continuous motion, making one strip. Coil the strip into a rose. Use cilantro for leaves.

175

Cucumber pinwheels can be made by cutting 6 or 8 V-shaped grooves along the cucumber lengthwise, spaced equally all around the cucumber. Slice ⅛ inch thick crosswise.

Pineapple makes an excellent "flower" for garnishing. Simply place a cherry tomato or maraschino cherry in the center of a canned pineapple ring. You can also create a "bow tie" by cutting a canned pineapple ring into wedges. Place two wedges point-to-point and lay a cherry in the middle.

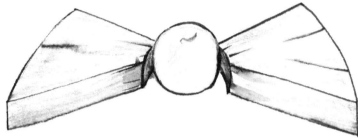

Lemon slices, lemon wedges, or a lemon half can be used as a garnish. To make the lemon half more attractive, cut the edge zigzag and place a maraschino cherry in the center.

Radish fans are pretty as a garnish. Trim off both ends of the radish, lay sideways, and make parallel cuts ⅛ inch apart and two-thirds of the way through the radish. Sprinkle with salt and refrigerate for 30 minutes. (Salt will soften the radish.) Spread fan gently.

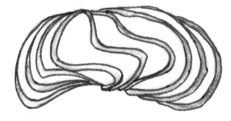

176

Carrots can be made into pinwheels following the instructions given for cucumber pinwheels. You can also make carrot roses. Choose a very large carrot. Peel and cut a ¾-inch piece from the thick end. With a paring knife (a) cut a triangle in the center; (b) cut a pentagon around the triangle; (c) make 7 cuts around the outer edge; (d) carve out some of the carrot along each cut to form petals.

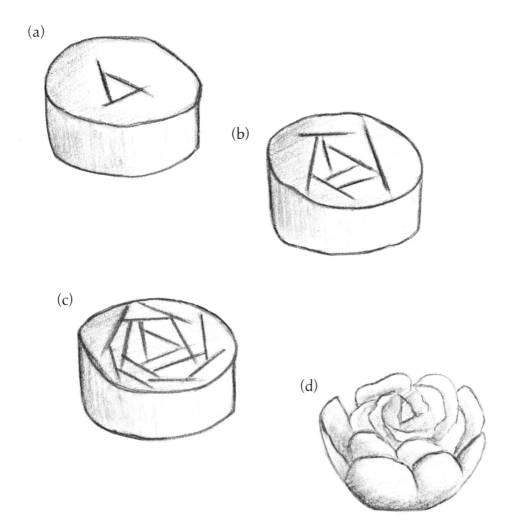

(a)

(b)

(c)

(d)

Cooked leafy vegetables, such as fresh spinach, watercress, lettuce, and Chinese cabbage, can also be served as garnishes. Either parboil in salted water containing 1 to 2 tablespoons vegetable oil per pound of vegetable, or stir-fry for 1 minute (stir-fry Chinese cabbage for 4 minutes). Drain and place the vegetable on a serving plate and top with cooked meat, poultry, or seafood. The vegetable serves as a "doily," making the dish more attractive and giving the illusion that there is more meat. In this case, the garnish is especially delicious because it has been flavored by the rich meat sauce.

CHINESE TEA

Tea is the national drink of China. The numerous kinds of Chinese tea can be grouped into three main categories: fermented, semifermented, and unfermented. Tea leaves from the same shrub can be treated differently to make any of these types of tea.

Fermented tea is black tea (Chinese call it red tea). After the leaves are picked and dried, they go through an oxidation or fermentation process and finally are fired in big ovens or firing machines. Black tea has a rich, soothing aroma.

Unfermented tea is green tea. The leaves are put into firing machines immediately after they are picked to prevent them from fermenting. The tea retains its green color along with a natural and refreshing fragrance. Dragon Well, considered the best green tea, is usually served at banquets.

Semifermented tea, such as Oolong, has a flavor halfway between black and green teas.

In each of these categories, many kinds of tea are available scented with flower blossoms or flavored with fruit. For example, litchee and rose teas are fermented, chrysanthemum and narcissus teas are unfermented, while jasmine tea is slightly fermented.

Tea is most often served hot. Preheat a clean porcelain teapot by rinsing with boiling water. Add ½ to 1 teaspoon tea leaves for each cup (depending upon how strong you like your tea). Next, pour boiling water over the tea leaves and cover. Let steep for 5 minutes. Sometimes tea leaves are placed in individual cups equipped with a cover to permit the tea to brew right in the cup.

Tea can be served on any occasion or at any time of day. In China, a guest is always offered tea upon arrival. Tea is traditionally served at the end of the meal but it may also be served during the meal.

DINNER WINE

The Chinese call all alcoholic beverages, including liquors, wine (酒) and serve them with dinner. Rice wine is one of the most common dinner wines in China. Although rice is the main ingredient, these wines differ widely in quality and taste because of the manufacturing methods, purity of ingredients, and length of time they are aged. **Shaohsing,** considered the best rice wine, resembles whisky in color. It should be warmed before serving.

Kaoliang, a distilled liquor, is made from millet. It is colorless, volatile, and extremely strong. I was told once that "to swallow one gulp of warm Kaoliang is like having a ball of fire roll down your throat." I always remember the warning. Whenever Kaoliang is offered, I just sip a little, trying not to taste it.

Chu Yeh Ching Liqueur is made from wheat, millet, green lentil, and herbs. It comes in a decorative porcelain bottle and is believed to have therapeutic value.

Wan Fu, a white wine produced and bottled in France, is not an authentic Chinese wine. However, according to the label, it is "produced from select and sumptuous grapes to complement all delicate Oriental dishes." Many of my students enjoy serving it with Chinese meals because it is closer to the taste they are accustomed to.

In a Western meal, dinner wine is chosen to complement the entrée. Since Chinese dinners always include more than one main dish, it would be difficult to complement each dish with a different wine. Therefore use your own judgment when choosing a beverage. Whatever you decide, it will not make your Chinese dinner less authentic.

MENU PLANNING

Menu planning is vital to a successful dinner, whether for two or twenty. The art of Chinese menu planning lies in blending and harmonizing aroma, taste, texture, and color. Delicate flavors should be offset by robust ones; spicy dishes should be complemented by bland ones; soft foods should be paired with crisp ones; and pale dishes should be accented by richly-colored ones. In short, "balance" is the key.

The main difference between a Western meal and a Chinese meal is that the former has a single entrée, while the latter includes several main dishes. In Western cuisines, when you have more guests, you increase the quantity; in Chinese cuisine, you increase the variety as well as quantity.

To plan a Chinese meal, you could start with a stir-fried meat (beef or pork) and vegetable dish, followed by chicken, fish, bean curd, pork or beef, shrimp, duck, crab, and so on (in any preferred order). While you are considering the main ingredients, keep in mind that the different cooking methods play a very important role in the aroma, taste, texture, and color of your presentations. Try to use different cooking methods. Stir-fried dishes should be limited to one or two. Here are several well-planned Chinese menus:

Suggested Menu for 2 to 4

Deep-Fried Wontons (¼ to ½ recipe)
with Hot Mustard and Sweet & Sour Sauce
Tomato Egg Drop Soup
Szechwan Eggplant
Steamed Fish
Stir-Fried Beef with Snow Peas
Boiled Rice
Spun Apples

Main ingredients: Ground pork, tomato, egg, eggplant, fish, beef, and snow peas.

Cooking methods: Deep-frying, boiling, braising, steaming, and stir-frying.

Aroma: Delicate flavors (soup and fish) offset by robust flavors (hot mustard, sweet & sour sauce, and Szechwan eggplant).

Taste: Spicy dishes (hot mustard and Szechwan eggplant) complemented by bland dishes (soup and fish).

Texture: Soft foods (tomato, eggplant, fish, and beef) paired with crisp foods (deep-fried wontons and snow peas).

Color: Pale dish (fish) accented by richly-colored dishes (beef with snow peas and tomato egg drop soup).

Suggested Menu for 6 to 8

Deep-Fried Shrimp Balls
Chicken and Dried Mushroom Soup
Cucumber Salad*
Crabmeat with Chinese Cabbage
Sweet and Sour Pork
Stir-Fried Beef with Broccoli
Roast Duck
Boiled Rice*
Almond Float*

Suggested Chinese Banquet Menu for 10 to 12

Cold dishes:
Tangy Cabbage*
Braised Star Anise Beef and Eggs
Smoked Chicken

Hot dishes:
Stir-Fried Beef with Asparagus
Lobster Cantonese
Abalone with Chinese Cabbage
Szechwan Crisp Duck
Twice-Cooked Pork
Sweet and Sour Whole Fish
Boiled Rice**
Birds' Nest Soup

Dessert:
Eight-Treasure Rice Pudding

Suggested Buffet Menu for 20

Egg Rolls with Shredded Chicken*
Beer Duck
Catsup Shrimp*
Stuffed Spareribs*
Braised Star Anise Beef and Eggs
Shredded Pork with Spicy Sauce*
Foil-Wrapped Chicken Slices**
Sweet and Sour Radishes*
Stir-Fried Chinese Cabbage**
Assorted Chow Mein*
Almond Cookies

* Double the recipe in this book.
** Triple the recipe in this book.

There is much more to menu planning than just cooking. First decide what to cook, read all the recipes well in advance. Make a shopping list and shop a day ahead. Jot down your menu and time to prepare each recipe. If you are planning a big party, cook all do-ahead recipes (indicated in the **Tip** section of each recipe) a day in advance. Even for a stir-fried dish that is better cooked at the last minute, you can cut the meat and vegetables, mix the sauce the day before, and refrigerate. If you carry out your well-laid plans step by step, by the time your guests arrive, you will be able to relax and enjoy the meal with them.

CHINESE TABLE SETTINGS
AND SERVING TIPS

For Westerners, half the fun and fascination of Chinese cuisine is the way the meal is served. For everyday family-style meals, the individual place setting includes a pair of chopsticks, a rice bowl, and a small dish for dipping sauce or for discarded bones and shells. If soup is served, add a soup spoon. All cooked dishes are placed in the center of the table at the same time. Boiled rice is always served in the individual bowls. The soup may be sipped throughout the meal. Fresh fruit is served at the end of the meal.

For a Chinese banquet, a round table seating 10 to 12 people is used. The host and hostess sit with their backs to the kitchen door (or to the direction from which the food will be brought) while the guests of honor sit opposite them. In this way the guests are not disturbed by the servant or waiter bringing in the food. Each place setting includes a pair of chopsticks (ivory ones are appropriate for a banquet), a small individual plate (7 to 8 inches in diameter), a porcelain soup spoon with a small dish to rest it on, a soup bowl (smaller than rice bowl, about 3½ inches in diameter), a small dish (3 inches in diameter) for sauce, and a wine cup or glass.

The table decorations are modest; centerpieces are not used since food is the main attraction. In fact, before the guests are seated, the center of the table is usually occupied by an elaborately arranged plate of assorted cold meats and vegetables of various colors and textures. As each course is placed in the center of the table, the guests help themselves, using their own chopsticks or serving spoons. Emptied serving dishes are removed from the table as new ones arrive.

Chinese table manners are very different from Western manners. Food is seldom passed. Since chopsticks are an extension of one's arm, each guest can reach from 3 to 4 feet across the table. Some banquet tables have a built-in lazy Susan in the center for easier serving.

In the past, the Chinese did not use napkins; instead they used hot, moist sterilized hand towels. Fresh towels were brought out by a servant or waiter throughout the meal. Today, because of Western influence, both paper and linen napkins are often used.

Buffet-style meals are adapted from the West. The Chinese have found that this is a wonderful way to entertain a large group of people.

When East meets West, you should adapt to fit the situation. You do not have to adhere completely to Chinese customs, but it is fun to learn about them and to use those customs you enjoy.

LIST OF RECIPES

INDEX